Advancing Wood Architecture

In light of environmental challenges architecture is facing, wood is no longer regarded as outmoded, nostalgic and rooted in the past, but increasingly recognised as one of the most promising building materials for the future. Recent years have seen unprecedented innovation of new technologies for advancing wood architecture.

Advancing Wood Architecture offers a comprehensive overview of the new architectural possibilities that are enabled by cutting-edge computational technologies in wood construction. It provides both an overarching architectural understanding and in-depth technological information through built projects and the works of four leading design research groups in Europe. The projects presented include large-scale, permanent buildings such as the ETH Arch_Tec_Lab building in Zurich, Switzerland; the Landesgartenschau Exhibition Hall near Stuttgart, Germany; and the Boiler House in Hooke Park, England; as well as built research prototypes investigating additive robotic fabrication, folded plate structures and meteorosensitive building skins.

Illustrated in full colour, the book showcases the latest technological developments in design computation, simulation and digital fabrication together with an architectural, engineering and manufacturing perspective, offering an outlook towards novel spatial and constructional opportunities of a material with unrivalled ecological virtues.

Achim Menges is a registered architect and professor at the University of Stuttgart, Germany, where he is the founding director of the Institute for Computational Design. Currently he is also Visiting Professor in Architecture at Harvard University's Graduate School of Design, USA.

Tobias Schwinn is a research associate and doctoral candidate at the Institute for Computational Design at the University of Stuttgart, Germany. In his research he is focusing on the integration of robotic fabrication and computational design processes.

Oliver David Krieg is a research associate and doctoral candidate at the Institute for Computational Design at the University of Stuttgart, Germany. His research aims to investigate the architectural potentials of robotic fabrication in wood construction.

"This remarkable book showcases what architects could create with wood today using the latest computational design and robotic fabrication technologies. It features innovative wood architecture designed – and made – by four leading research groups in Europe. Rethinking wood from a computational perspective, they point to a variety of new ways in which this humble yet incredible material could be used in contemporary architecture."

– *Branko Kolarevic, University of Calgary, Canada*

Advancing Wood Architecture

A computational approach

Edited by Achim Menges, Tobias Schwinn
and Oliver David Krieg

Routledge
Taylor & Francis Group

LONDON AND NEW YORK

First published 2017
by Routledge
2 Park Square, Milton Park, Abingdon, Oxon OX14 4RN

and by Routledge
711 Third Avenue, New York, NY 10017

Routledge is an imprint of the Taylor & Francis Group, an informa business

British Library Cataloguing-in-Publication Data
A catalogue record for this book is available from the British Library

Library of Congress Cataloging-in-Publication Data
Names: Menges, Achim, author. | Schwinn, Tobias, author. | Krieg, Oliver David, author.
Title: Advancing wood architecture : a computational approach / Achim Menges, Tobias Schwinn, and Oliver David Krieg.
Description: New York : Routledge, 2016. | Includes bibliographical references and index.
Identifiers: LCCN 2015047854| ISBN 9781138932982 (hb : alk. paper) | ISBN 9781138932999 (pb : alk. paper) | ISBN 9781315678825 (ebook)
Subjects: LCSH: Building, Wooden--Technological innovations. | Building, Wooden--History--21st century.
Classification: LCC NA4110 .M46 2016 | DDC 721/.0448--dc23
LC record available at http://lccn.loc.gov/2015047854

ISBN: 978-1-138-93298-2 (hbk)
ISBN: 978-1-138-93299-9 (pbk)
ISBN: 978-1-315-67882-5 (ebk)

Typeset in Minion Pro
by Fakenham Prepress Solutions, Fakenham, Norfolk NR21 8NN

Printed by Bell & Bain Ltd, Glasgow.

− CONTENTS −

No question, there are myriad books on timber construction and wood architecture. Their scope spans from technical construction manuals to literature focusing on the history and cultural relevance of this building material. However, since we started working with wood at the Institute for Computational Design several years ago, we felt that a particular book was missing from this extensive range: a book that contextualizes the remarkable characteristics and qualities of wood within the contemporary context of digital design, simulation and fabrication; a book that does not merely look at advances in CAD/CAM timber construction from the vantage point of automation, precision and workflow, but rather in the spirit of architectural exploration and innovation. In a nutshell, a book that would locate the intersection between what arguably is one of the oldest building materials with the very latest cyber-physical enabling technologies as a starting point for architectural enquiry.

With the completion of a major research undertaking, the EU funded 'Robotics in Timber Manufacturing' project that resulted in the novel wood plate structure showcased in the Landesgartenschau Exhibition Hall building in Schwäbisch Gmünd, Germany, we had a renewed incentive to step back and reflect on the project outcome in relation to the larger developments in the field. This spawned the idea of instigating a broader conversation with like-minded researchers, architects, and engineers in the form of a one-day symposium and related publication, focusing on the ramifications of cutting-edge digital technologies and the spatial as well as constructional potentials they may offer for architecture.

We were delighted to find out that a number of our most innovative and esteemed colleagues from renowned international institutions shared our enthusiasm for the topic at hand, and that they generously agreed to present and discuss their highly accomplished work. The *Advancing Wood Architecture* Symposium took place at the German Museum of Architecture on 27 March 2015. We envisioned this event to be both an exchange of overarching thoughts on advancing wood architecture, as well as a discussion of specific research undertakings and related building projects in greater technical detail. This twofold concept, the insights it offered, and the fascination it sparked is very much at the heart of the book in your hands.

Achim Menges, Tobias Schwinn, Oliver David Krieg

— A C K N O W L E D G E M E N T S —

The editors would like to express their genuine gratitude to all the contributors to this book: Axel Kilian (Princeton University) for his insightful foreword and his fine summary of the conclusive discussion on architectural perspectives at the *Advancing Wood Architecture* Symposium, as well as Johan Bettum (Städelschule Frankfurt) for injecting fresh, inspiring and critical thoughts into this conversation; Fabio Gramazion, Matthias Kohler, and Jan Willmann for their astute contribution, and Volker Helm, Michael Knauss, Thomas Kohlhammer, and Aleksandra Anna Apolinarska for their description of two highly advanced projects (all: Gramazio Kohler Research, ETH Zürich); Yves Weinand for his great account of past and present wood innovation, as well as Christopher Robeller, Sina Nabaei, and Olivier Baverel for insightful research summaries (all: IBOIS, EPFL Lausanne); Martin Self for his striking perspective, and Glen Stellmacher and Yingzi Wang for their forward-looking projects and texts (all: Design & Make, Architectural Association London). In addition the editors would like to thank Manfred Grohmann and Jan Knippers, as well as Müllerblaustein Holzbau and Amann Holzbau for sharing their insights on engineering and manufacturing perspectives of wood architecture.

The generous support of Peter Schmal (Director German Museum of Architecture) in hosting the symposium at his museum, as well as the financial contribution of the sponsors to making this event possible, are sincerely acknowledged by the editors. Equally, they would like to thank all student assistants for the tremendous effort in helping with the organisational matters of the symposium and the book. A special thank-you also goes to Francesca Ford for her great support of this book project, and to Trudy Varcianna for her help and patience in turning it into reality. Finally, the editors would also express their gratitude to the University of Stuttgart for providing an excellent academic environment in which this line of work can thrive.

Axel Kilian

School of Architecture, Princeton University, USA

MODELS for computation, design processes, and their physical implementations have coevolved for centuries. Different disciplines developed numeric, geometric, and material aspects but at the core stands the externalization of an idea into a material construct in various forms of abstractions from representations of numeric systems to dimensionally scaled architectural artifacts. Wood as a material has always played an important role as an easily shapeable yet lasting resource, equally adept at embodying abstract tokens, construction aids such as ship curves, scale models, and full scale architecture. The transition from analogue computation embodied in the material to numeric based digital systems led to the loss of much of the implicit knowledge that now has to be reintegrated into material aware work flows and design processes. The development of numerically controlled machining triggered the development of computer assisted design (CAD) systems and now the adaptation of sensor enabled robotic systems triggers a rethinking of design processes and geometric representations to establish a closer link between computational model and material realm. Wood has evolved from being an easily available material to being the seed of a renewed interest in material aware design processes, which reintegrate the awareness of the intricacies and complexity of a material known for thousands of years into computational processes. In tracing out the co-development of computing processes and computer-numerically controlled fabrication, the discussion of the contemporary relationship of computation and the material wood is put into context.

From analogue to digital computing

WOOD has a long history of use for architectural models such as in Sangallo's and Michelangelo's wood models for St Peter's, essentially physical renderings and geometric prototypes. Simultaneously computation became more abstract through the further development of numeric and mathematical methods in parallel to the increasing demands of early industrialization such as expanding trade networks that relied on the calculation of tide tables for ship access into harbours. The need to increase manufacturing output spurred the first instance of a pre-digitized form of data controlled manufacturing by Joseph-Marie Jacquard in 1802 with his punch card controlled weaving machine (Campbell-Kelly & Aspray, 1996) (Figure F.1).

It still took another 20 years for a proposal for a computing machine to emerge. Charles Babbage became familiar with table processing techniques developed by De Prony in France (Campbell-Kelly & Aspray, 1996), based on breaking down complex calculations into simple addition and subtraction processes, allowing minimally educated human computers to calculate the numerical tables. Through the translation of these methods into mechanical form Babbage developed the difference machine, an analogue hand-powered specific purpose computer. He also designed the analytical engine, the first general purpose computing machine. Both expanded the scope of computation towards more general purpose calculations by using the punch card system that was introduced by Jacquard. A first theory of programming was developed by Augusta Ada, Countess of Lovelace in response to the possibilities of the analytical engine (Menabrea, 1843).

The real time need for computation became more pressing in the technologically accelerated context of war. The earliest real-time computation instances were naval range finders for the computation of gun angles. They were based on a suite of optical measurements pulled together in early analogue computers that used spinning disc units for integration (Mindell, 2002). Only around a decade later the ENIAC (Electronic Numerical Integrator and Computer) at the University of Pennsylvania became one of the first electronic computers using standardized computing units that were rewired for each new calculation operation, which can be seen as a form of proto programming (Figure F.2).

Connecting computing and making

In the 1950s the Massachusetts Institute of Technology (MIT) developed the first instance of a computer numerical control (CNC) machine with the (Automatically Programmed Tool) APT system linking the whirlwind computer to a servomechanism controlled milling machine (Ross, 1959). It is interesting to note that, while different in the details, the process is remarkably similar to today's CNC processes – an

Figure F.1

Woven silk portrait of Joseph-Marie Jacquard, *À la Mémoire de J.M. Jacquard, Né à Lyon le 7 Juillet 1752, Mort le 7 Août 1834*, executed in 1839 on the programmable Jacquard loom by Didier Petit et Cie, Lyon.

abstracted series of steps to produce the instructions for the machine that is very detached from the material and design process itself.

The invention of anthropomorphic mechanical arms has a long history in automata. In 1938 the first proposals emerged for their deployment in the industry with the Pollard painting arm, followed a few decades later by the first universally applicable industrial arm, the Unimate (Moran, 2007) (Figure F.3). The further parallel development of servo control electronics

Figure F.3
The Unimate was the first robotic arm used in industry.

and computational geometry ultimately enabled the development of robotic manufacturing technologies in the 1960s and their adoption in construction, first in Japan, and later in 2005 in architecture by Gramazio Kohler Research at ETH Zürich, and soon after by other institutes to name only a few, the Technische Universität in Vienna, the Harvard Graduate School of Design, the University of Michigan, and the Institute for Computational Design in Stuttgart (Kohler, Gramazio & Willmann, 2014).

Beginning in the 1960s, in response to the availability of these new CNC capabilities, CAD design systems were developed in order to make it possible to generate numerical data from complex geometry. Ivan Sutherland pioneered one of the first design systems in 1963 with his sketchpad thesis (Sutherland, 1963) (Figure F.4).

Also in the 1960s methods for modelling complex curves were developed independently by Paul de Casteljau at Citroën and Pierre Bézier at Peugeot in France (Farin, 2002). These were the first numerical methods for how designers had drawn curves for wooden ship hulls for centuries. Wood was commonly used in ship curves, which allowed a quasi-parametric adjustability of curvature through the embodied moment resistance of the wood ruler bent by set screws or weights. The further development of the mathematical curvature model led to NURBS (non-uniform rational basis spline) modelling that enabled the wide use of digitally modelled curved surfaces.

Today, material behaviours are fed back into computational processes such as in the chair example by the author (Kilian, 2006) (Figure F.5), where the curvature and bending resistance are an integral part of the snap fit interlocking nature of the sequential assembly of the structure into

Figure F.4

TX-2 Operating Area. The Sketchpad was a man-machine graphical communication system created by Ivan Edward Sutherland.

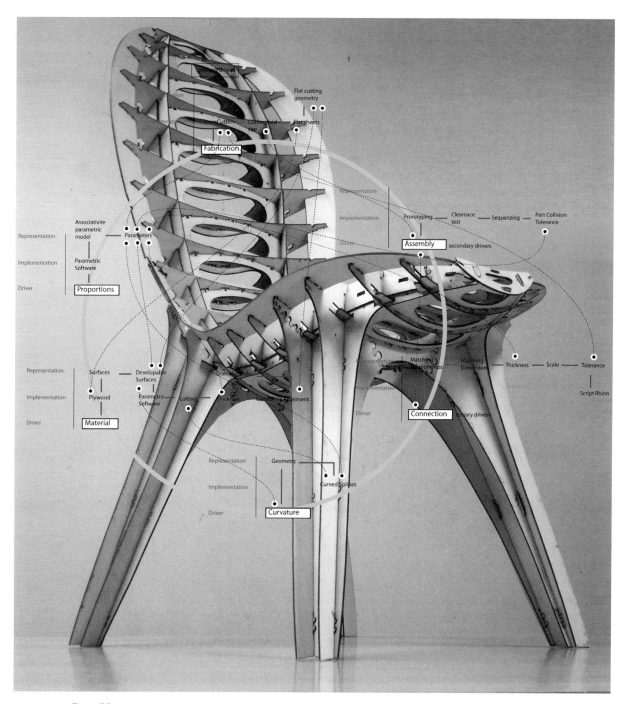

Figure F.5

The Plywood chair exemplifies today's possibility of feedback between design computation, material behaviour and digital fabrication.

the overall chair. At the same time we are moving into a post mechanical time, where feedback and control systems begin to take over the role of analogue mechanics, opening up the possibility to conceive of the interaction between machine material manipulation and human operator as an open process (Johns, Kilian & Foley, 2014).

Outlook

THE biological process that creates wood – from a seedling to a full grown tree – can produce building size constructs such as a sequoia, sustained only by local resources and solar energy, which makes one appreciate the complex, integrative and ecologically embedded character of biological growth. As more is understood about these natural processes, wood as a material is appreciated more for its intricate anatomy and inherent qualities. Employing computation as an interface between the digital and the physical world, new research initiatives are beginning to tap into this pool of materially innate design possibilities, exploring new computational approaches to wood in architecture as presented in this book.

References

Campbell-Kelly, M. & Aspray, W. (1996). *Computer: A History of the Information Machine*. New York: Westview Press.

Farin, G.E. (2002). A Histroy of Curves and Surfaces in CAGD. In G.E. Farin, J. Hoschek & M.-S. Kim (eds), *Handbook of Computer Aided Geometric Design* (pp. 1–22). Amsterdam, Boston, MA: Elsevier.

Johns, R., Kilian, A. & Foley, N. (2014). Design Approaches through Augmented Materiality and Embodied Computation. In W. McGee & M. Ponce de Leon (eds), *Robotic Fabrication in Architecture, Art and Design 2014*. Cham: Springer International Publishing.

Kilian, A. (2006). *Design Exploration through Bidirectional Modeling of Constraints*. Massachusetts Institute of Technology PhD Thesis.

Kohler, M., Gramazio, F. & Willmann, J. (2014). *The Robotic Touch: How Robots Change Architecture, Gramazio & Kohler Research ETH Zürich 2005–2013*. Zurich: Park Books.

Menabrea, L.F. (1843). *Sketch of the Analytical Engine Invented by Charles Babbage* [translated, and appended with additional notes, by Augusta Ada, Countess of Lovelace], London: Richard & John Taylor.

Mindell, D.A. (2002). *Johns Hopkins Studies in the History of Technology. Between Human and Machine: Feedback, Control, and Computing before Cybernetics*. Baltimore, MD: The Johns Hopkins University Press.

Moran, M.E. (2007). Evolution of Robotic Arms. *Journal of Robotic Surgery*, 1(2), 103–111.

Ross, D.T. (1959). *The Automatically Programmed Tool System. Volume I, General Description of the Apt System*. Cambridge, MA: Servomechanisms Laboratory MIT.

Sutherland, I.E. (1963) Sketch Pad: A Man-machine Graphical Communication System. In *AFIPS Conference Proceedings 23* (pp. 323–328).

An introduction

Achim Menges, Tobias Schwinn, Oliver David Krieg

Institute for Computational Design, University of Stuttgart, Germany

It is a question of surrendering to the wood, then following where it leads by connecting operations to a materiality, instead of imposing a form upon a matter: what one addresses is less a matter submitted to laws than a materiality possessing a nomos. One addresses less a form capable of imposing properties upon a matter than material traits of expression constituting affects.

(Deleuze & Guattari, 1987)

WOOD is a fascinating building material for architecture. It embodies a rich history and has deep cultural roots, while at the same time providing striking prospects for the future built environment, which mainly stem from the confluence of two important factors: the ever-expanding design, simulation and fabrication possibilities enabled by computation on the one hand, and wood's virtues as one of the few ecologically sound building materials on the other. In the light of both the rapid technological advances we are experiencing and the severe environmental challenges architecture is facing, wood can no longer be understood as an outdated material with inferior properties and idiosyncratic characteristics as compared to industrially produced building materials. Instead, it is increasingly regarded as a most promising building material for the future with unrivalled environmental advantages.

Biological building material

TODAY, about 30% of all land area worldwide is covered with forests. Of these 3.9 billion hectares, about 57% are found in developing countries (Wegener & Zimmer, 2003). This poses a challenge in regards to sustainable silviculture as it is practiced by most developed nations (Figure 0.1). However, with the right policies and rules in place, this would constitute a vast, potentially fully renewable resource. As wood grows as the biological tissue of trees, its production primarily consumes solar – that is natural – energy during photosynthesis, even converting carbon

Figure 0.1

Natural resource wood: wood constitutes one of the very few fully renewable and naturally grown building materials, which results in unrivalled environmental characteristics. The image shows harvested timber floating on a river in Savonlinna, Finland.
Bjorn Svensson, Science Photo Library

dioxide into oxygen during this process. As a result of the natural growth, even when taking today's heavily industrial wood processing into account, wood products hold a very low level of embodied energy (Alcorn, 1996) together with a positive carbon footprint (Kolb, 2008).

Wood's outstanding ecological characteristics are demonstrated, for example, by the fact that the production of a panel with a given compressive strength in wood requires 500 times less energy than in steel (Gordon, 2003). In addition, wood as a building material also offers a remarkable synergy of environmental and structural performance. In fact, as wood is a natural composite material made from cellulose fibres with a high percentage of cavities, it is the structurally most capable insulating building material we have at our disposal (Figure 0.2). While offering a significantly smaller heat transfer coefficient, it has almost the same compressive strength as concrete (Cheret & Seidel, 2013), and it is lighter than steel for the same tensile loading capacity.

Craft to computation

FOR many centuries wood has been the single most important building resource. Until the end of the eighteenth century, more than 80% of all buildings were timber structures (Cheret & Seidel, 2013). In these preindustrial times the inherent heterogeneity and natural variance of wood was accepted and effectively utilized. The intricate structural differences in the raw material were employed for specific building elements through manual wood-working techniques. These slow yet ingenious fabrication methods, which were developed and adapted over hundreds of years, allowed to precisely cut and bend the harvested log following the natural grain direction. As a result, the craft-based design and construction techniques were in close relation to the available material and its specific, highly anisotropic characteristics.

With the dawn of industrialization, the predominance of wood architecture became increasingly challenged by synthetic materials like iron, steel, concrete and others. As technological advances introduced new building materials and production processes, the traditional understanding of wood as a natural material became questioned by both the availability of more homogenous materials with precisely defined properties and more normative

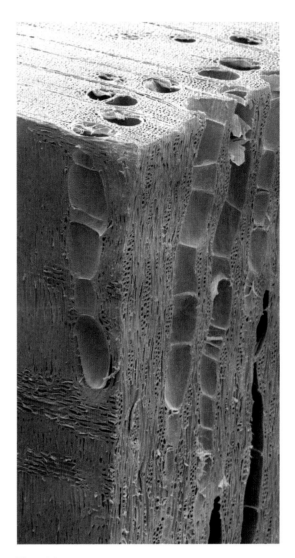

Figure 0.2

Biological building material: wood grows as the functional tissue of trees, which results in the differentiated cellular anatomy that determines its material characteristics. The image shows a coloured scanning electron micrograph (SEM) of a block of wood from an elm tree (*Ulmus procera*). The top of the block is a transverse section and the sides are longitudinal sections. Xylem vessels (larger tubes) are seen in the wood. The xylem transports water and mineral nutrients from the roots throughout the plant.

Power and Syred, Science Photo Library

design and engineering approaches (Figure 0.3). Today emerging digital technologies herald a renewed possibility for material-specific design approaches that were increasingly lost over the last two centuries.

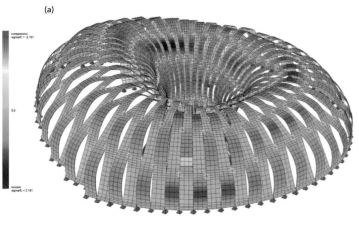

Figure 0.3

Computational design and simulation: advances in design computation and simulation allow exploring material specific characteristics of wood as a generative driver in design. The image shows the simulation (a) of a bending active structure based on elastically formed plywood lamellas (b).

ICD/ITKE University of Stuttgart

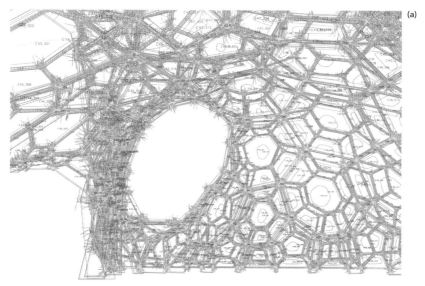

Figure 0.4

Computational design and robotic fabrication: advances in design computation and robotic fabrication enable a direct feedback between manufacturing constraints and form generation, (a) which allows exploring novel constructional systems and (b) spatial articulation for wood architecture.

ICD/ITKE University of Stuttgart

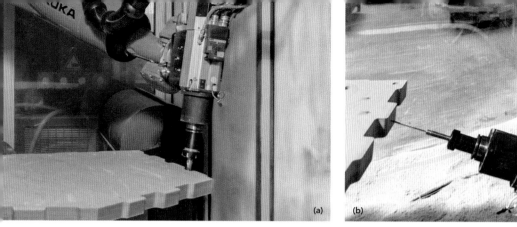

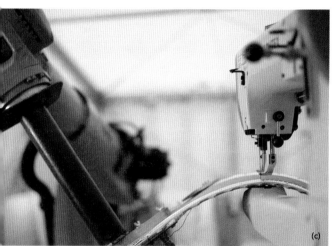

Figure 0.5

Robotic wood fabrication: in contrast to task-specific CAM machines that have been used in wood fabrication for several decades, industrial robots constitute more universally usable and flexible fabrication set-ups. Subtractive robotic wood fabrication includes for example (a) 7-axis milling and (b) robotic drilling. Examples of additive robotic wood fabrication are (c) robotic plywood sewing and (d) assembly of timber elements into building parts.
ICD/ITKE University of Stuttgart

Recent years have seen the unprecedented innovation of new technologies for the advancement of wood architecture. This includes new approaches to design computation and simulation (Figure 0.4), as well as new technologies for digital wood scanning and robotic timber manufacturing (Figure 0.5). Employing computation to tap into the intricate and multifaceted design potential latent in wood enables the development of constructional systems that no longer need to be derivatives of long-established and standardized building systems and elements.

Form or matter

THE discourse on technological advancements of wood architecture tends to revolve around two distinct approaches: One approach recognizes the anatomy of the tree trunk as a form-defining element, considering its directionality, anisotropy and heterogeneous make-up, and reflecting this in the constructional logic and tectonic articulation. The other seeks to homogenize the material as engineered wood products, which are viewed as more generic building matter that still maintain some of the advantages of wood. Technological progress has not only made it easier to break-up the natural log into required parts, but also to reorganize its substance into new wood-based products that barely resemble the tree from which they originated.

Over the last century wood processing and manufacturing has developed the ability to decompose and restructure the material on a cellular level, with the aim to make the material technically more manageable and almost limitless in its geometric articulation (Blumer, 2014). The advances in industrial wood processing and engineering are most prominently visible in the transition from linear wooden elements that still resemble the natural growth direction and functional morphology of the tree, to large plate products such as plywood, fibre boards or cross-laminated timber. Through this reorganization and reassembly of the material, wood has expanded its constructional possibilities beyond beam and grid structures towards plate and surface structures, offering manifold opportunities for new architectural application.

At the same time, traditional craft techniques of working with the idiosyncrasies of wood are experiencing a revival through digital technologies. The tacit knowledge passed down through generations of carpenters can now be augmented with computational means, ranging from computer-controlled fabrication to full cyber-physical scanning and production systems that can respond to the unique grain and make-up of each single work piece. The technology for digitizing the individual anatomy of each log is already very much in place, as most advanced sawmills use scanning techniques to algorithmically define cut-up patterns for maximum yield and profit (Figure 0.6). While today the related datasets are still mostly lost by the time the wood leaves the saw mill, big data strategies together with ever more advanced scanning technologies, such as computer tomography, will allow the inclusion of specific anatomic information in design in the not too distant future (Figure 0.7). This potential design

Figure 0.6

Digital wood processing: today's saw mills and wood processing extensively utilizes digital technology, for example to scan logs and to algorithmically determine their most profitable break up.

Metsä Wood

Figure 0.7

Log computer tomography: advanced wood scanning techniques include (a) computer tomography, (b) which results in comprehensive, three-dimensional anatomic datasets of the log.

Udo Sauter, FVA Freiburg

feedback with digitizing technologies and simulation capabilities allows viewing the natural variability of wood through a totally different lens, taking inspiration from the pre-industrial utilization of wood while at the same time injecting wood with entirely new possibilities.

Today, designers, architects and engineers can tap into a vast pool of possibilities for rethinking wood, either by employing the material's natural traits and characteristics as a design driver, or by taking full advantage of the reconfiguration of the material through advanced processing and fabrication processes. Neither one of these two approaches is less interesting than the other, nor are they necessarily mutually exclusive. The goal of this book is to showcase the architectural perspectives latent in both directions, as well as the multifaceted ways in which they can be combined.

Advancing wood architecture

This book aims to provide a comprehensive overview of the new architectural possibilities that are offered by cutting edge computational technologies in wood construction. It covers advanced research and related building projects, providing both an overarching architectural understanding and in-depth technological information through comprehensive, project-based descriptions. It brings the latest technological developments in design computation, simulation and digital fabrication together with an architectural, engineering and manufacturing perspective, offering an outlook towards novel spatial, constructional, and fabricational opportunities of a material with unrivalled ecological virtues.

The following chapters of the book present the work of four leading European research groups in the field. Their ongoing research in computational design and digital fabrication has significantly pushed the advancements of wood construction in architecture in recent years. Each is presented by an introduction of its overall research agenda and its approach towards the development and design of novel wood architecture. Complementing the overarching statements on the architectural, technological and ecological possibilities of advancing wood construction through computational technologies, each group will present two projects in greater detail. In this way the book aims at providing a unique combination of both an overarching architectural perspective and in-depth technological information through comprehensive, project-based descriptions.

In Part 1 Gramazio Kohler Research at ETH Zürich presents novel, interdisciplinary approaches for highly flexible and environmentally sound timber constructions. In their articles, the reciprocal relation between robotic fabrication and wood construction points the way to a future where renewable, possibly local, materials are given new architectural articulations and structural potential. With many years of experience in robotic additive manufacturing, as well as empirical experiments and prototyping, they not only unlock new opportunities for full-scale digital timber construction, but also expand the understanding of integrative computational design methodologies. The presented body of applied research mainly focuses on additive fabrication techniques of unique or standardized timber elements.

The research by the Timber Construction Laboratory IBOIS at the École Polytechnique Fédérale (EPFL), Lausanne, introduces a different facet of rethinking wood architecture. Their work employs flexibility and softness, attributes associated with textiles and fabrics that seem at first to contradict robust and static load bearing structures. In addition, the research also explores the structural capabilities of folded plate structures in conjunction with new fabrication technology. The group highlights how the reconsideration of established notions of timber structures becomes necessary in the context of environmental challenges that the building industry is facing. First prototypical results provide the conceptual framework for the development of novel approaches and methods for the design, simulation, analysis, and fabrication of timber fabric and plate structures in architecture.

Part 3 focuses on the work of the Institute for Computational Design (ICD) at the University of Stuttgart, introducing three research fields within wood architecture that integrate and combine fundamental material properties through computational design, simulation, and fabrication processes. On the one hand the research is based on the fact that as a naturally grown tissue, wood's material structure is defined by its growth process, thereby reflecting the biological requirements of trees. Using the resulting characteristics as design drivers for innovative architecture, fundamentally new fields of application can be explored. On the other hand, the material's machinability in combination with digital fabrication techniques defines another field of research that is presented through prototypical research projects.

The work of the Architectural Association (AA) School of Architecture's Design & Make Master of Architecture (MArch) programme, presented in Part 4, showcases material-based research that directly resulted from the institution's location within the woodland campus in the west of England. The history of Hooke Park, where experimentation with wood has a long tradition, served as a basis for innovative building prototypes that are developed and produced by students and researchers. The projects follow a research agenda that takes advantage of the specific local characteristics of timber: ranging from digitally cataloguing tree forms and applying Big Data strategies in order to match individual shapes contained in large databases and individually required joint geometries, to vision- and sensor-guided robotic machining that allows feedback between the material's anisotropic behaviour and the digital fabrication process not dissimilar to the hand-eye-touch coordination of the skilled human craftsman.

In Part 5 the previous presentation of research work is complemented by both a manufacturing perspective, reflecting on the view of two leading timber construction companies on the effects of digitalization and increasing automation on timber construction, and an engineering perspective based on a conversation with two internationally renowned structural engineers. By situating the presented work in a larger context of disciplinary discourse, the book concludes with a comprehensive assessment of the possibilities and challenges wood offers for advancing architecture.

References

Alcorn, A. (1996). *Embodied Energy Coefficients of Building Materials*. Wellington: Centre for Building Performance Research.

Blumer, H. (2014). Das Holz und seine Wege. In M. Rinke & J. Schwartz (eds), *Holz: Stoff oder Form: Transformation einer Konstruktionslogik* (1st edn). Sulgen: Niggli.

Cheret, P. & Seidel, A. (2013). Der neue Holzbau. In P. Cheret, K. Schwaner, & A. Seidel (eds), *Urbaner Holzbau: Handbuch und Planungshilfe* . Berlin: DOM Publishers.

Deleuze, G. & Guattari, F. (1987). *A Thousand Plateaus: Capitalism and Schizophrenia*. Minneapolis, MN: University of Minnesota Press.

Gordon, J.E. (2003). *Structures: or Why Things Don't Fall Down* (2nd edn). New York: Da Capo Press.

Kolb, J. (2008). *Systems in Timber Engineering: Loadbearing Structures and Component Layers*. Basel: Birkhäuser Basel.

Wegener, G. & Zimmer, F. (2003). Bauen mit Holz ist zukunftsfähiges Bauen. In T. Herzog, J. Natterer, R. Schweitzer, W. Winter, M. Volz & F. Zeitler (eds), *Edition Detail. Holzbau-Atlas* (4th edn). Basel: Birkhäuser.

PART ONE

Gramazio Kohler Research, ETH Zürich, Switzerland

1

New paradigms of the automatic
Robotic timber construction in architecture

Jan Willmann, Fabio Gramazio, Matthias Kohler
ETH Zürich, Gramazio Kohler Research, Switzerland

THE combination of pioneering robotic fabrication technology with the sustainable material wood points the way to a future where renewable, possibly local materials are given novel aesthetic and structural potential through bespoke automated robotic assembly methods. In their contribution, Jan Willmann, Fabio Gramazio and Matthias Kohler of Gramazio Kohler Research at ETH Zürich, present novel, interdisciplinary approaches for highly flexible and environmentally sound timber constructions. Through empirical experiments, they not only unlock new opportunities for full-scale digital timber construction, providing structural efficiency through a locally differentiated aggregation of material, but also foster the development of integrative computational design methodologies and techniques.

Automated assembly processes

IN robotic timber construction, new digital design processes and fabrication techniques allow non-standard assembly to become an increasingly interesting architectural avenue, departing from traditional and labour-intensive manufacturing processes. Indeed, despite strong advancements in timber prefabrication using widely available computer numerical control (CNC) systems, the timber construction sector is still characterised by a high proportion of manual assembly tasks. Together with the inherently limited flexibility and constrained working areas of conventional CNC machinery, this handicaps the field when trying to take advantage of the rapidly spreading trend to use complex digital design information directly as input for comprehensively automated construction processes. Here, robotic systems are extremely useful – not only can their use lead to significant time savings, but their ability to transfer computational design data directly to real-world assembly operations enables the fully automated construction of non-standard timber structures (Figures 1.1 and 1.2). In particular, their use opens up entirely new possibilities for future timber construction that is not limited by the same constraints – such as, for example, work-intensive joinery and/or additional scaffolding. Instead, the exploration of robotic timber construction outlines new opportunities for integral automated machining and assembly of building components and the (digital) integration of all additional processing into a unified fabrication system; its most evident and radical consequences are the ability to digitally oversee and control a large number of aspects of the design and construction (for instance the sequencing of the single elements and their assembly). Most importantly robotic systems feature the ability to freely manipulate and position building components in space (Figure 1.3). However, considering

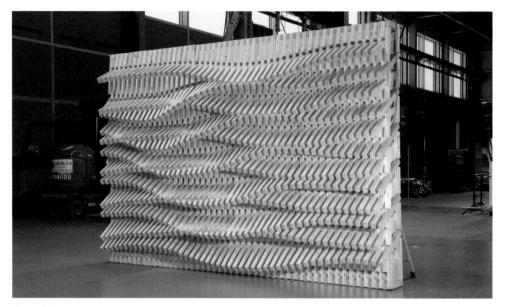

Figure 1.1
'The Sequential Wall' was one of the first projects to investigate the architectural and constructive potential of additive robotic timber fabrication. The interplay of many small parts results in a material system whose aesthetic and functional properties reach far beyond the single timber module.
Gramazio Kohler Research, ETH Zürich, 2008

Figure 1.2
The custom-built end-effector of the robot corresponds with custom export and design scripts that link the physical machine with digital data.
Gramazio Kohler Research, ETH Zürich, 2008

Figure 1.3 (facing page)
'The Stacked Pavilion' represents a further stage of development and is conceived as a temporary spatial structure and consists of 16 elements made from 372 wooden battens. The pavilion is fabricated from simple wooden battens by robotic cutting and positioning.
Gramazio Kohler Research, ETH Zürich, 2009

building-scale applications, such a fully integrated robotic assembly of complex timber structures is still in its infancy, and presents many theoretical, practical and methodological challenges to architecture.

In order to address these challenges, in 2008 the Gramazio Kohler Research group at ETH Zürich started a number of investigations into robotic assembly of complex timber structures. These explorations make an important step away from building with standard elements (such as, for example, bricks) to building with non-standard timber components, where both a novel aesthetic and a functional potential is liberated through the introduction of a minimal customisation of individual components (Gramazio & Kohler, 2008). Due to the fact that these components are not only robotically machined, but also assembled, the resulting structures combine the flexibility of individually fabricated, highly customised building parts with the advantages of additive mass production (Figure 1.4). As such, these structures can be fabricated without any need for repetition, at low cost and with a constant and controllable quality. The driving force of this approach is not the mere rationalisation of fabrication but the exploration of novel timber constructions, and their relation to the design freedom, the structural performance and the robotic assembly itself.

Starting initially from layer-based systems by robotically adding customised timber members into non-standard walls and structures, the research has substantially expanded during the last years towards the robotic aggregation of elements freely in space (Figure 1.5). Material is placed exactly where it is needed according to the digital blueprint and there is no need for repetition or standard construction routines, as it is usually required in any economic 'manual' build-up process. As such, this approach yields not only to minimal material waste but also additional material savings since there is no need to construct additional scaffolding or external building references.

Figure 1.4

'The Sequential Structure' expands the layered constructive system towards a spatial constructive system. The resulting shell structure (consisting of 26 individually fabricated structural components) enables a flexible response to local structural requirements and is based on a hanging chain model, developed in cooperation with the Block Research Group at ETH Zürich.

Gramazio Kohler Research, ETH Zürich, 2010

Figure 1.5
The building structure consists of 3,026 individual timber slats that were cut to length, automatically placed and glued by an industrial robot.
Gramazio Kohler Research, ETH Zürich, 2010

This unique approach on spatial timber assemblies is particularly explored in the framework of the SNSF NRP 66 'Resource Wood' research programme and created first experimental demonstrations, which are presented in the first part of this chapter. Subsequently, this article will discuss the industrial implementation of research, and a first large-scale demonstration, called 'The Sequential Roof'. Both endeavours required many innovations (including the development of novel computational design and construction processes, interfacing seamlessly with automated fabrication procedures), and successfully illustrated the potentials of comprehensively automated assembly processes, fostering profound changes in the design, performance and expression of architecture at building scale.

Advances in timber manufacturing

Despite the fact that architecture is constantly getting more complex, the building industry does not make effective use of modern computational fabrication technologies. In fact, it is still strongly driven by manual construction processes, which results in high costs, inconsistent work quality and significant waste of human and material resources. One reason for the low level of industrialisation of the building industry in comparison to other manufacturing industries, such as, for instance, the automotive industry, is the fact that typically building constructions are unique. As 'one of a kind' productions they are custom-built in accordance to individual needs and contexts. However, a particular case is presented by the timber construction sector, which through the arrival of digitally controlled joinery machines for automated manufacturing of timber construction components by the 1980s gained the possibility of a radical technological reorientation (Kuechle & Volkmann, 1986). Alongside the development of innovative, high-quality timber construction products, the associated transformation introduced a remarkable increase in flexibility and manufacturing productivity (Weinand & Buri, 2011). In the course of the recent shift towards digital production technology, research groups, such as, for instance, Gramazio Kohler Research (Gramazio, Kohler & Oesterle, 2010) and the Institute for Computational Design (ICD) (Schwinn, Krieg & Menges, 2012) have set up robotic research facilities for non-standard automated timber manufacturing in architecture. Here, a number of promising robotic manufacturing processes have been developed, resulting in robust, highly adaptable and sustainable timber constructions and building systems. Seen against this background, digital timber construction is fast becoming a mature technology (Bachmann et al., 2008), and is almost ready for large-scale assembly tasks. However, despite the use of automated robotic technology, a number of these prototypical structures are largely built through extensive machining of components and subsequent manual assembly processes (Schindler, 2009). This not only results in laborious fabrication routines and significant waste of human and material resources, but also heavily constrains the architectural exploration of the full potential of novel automated timber construction systems, and, ultimately, prevents robotic fabrication technology from spreading out into the timber sector on a larger scale.

Robotic timber construction

In the field of robotic timber construction there are only a few specific experiments and built demonstrations presently available (Figure 1.6). Our goal is therefore to foster constructive processes and case studies with the most realistic impact possible, and their transfer into building-scale solutions. Our research into robotic assembly of spatial timber structures, pursued in cooperation with the Bern University of Applied Sciences (Prof. Eduard Bachmann and Prof. Christophe Sigrist), offers a uniquely integral approach, addressing 1) assembly-driven design processes, 2) constructive systems, and 3) integrated robotic fabrication. The convergence of these three trajectories takes account of their overall capabilities and limitations regarding the physical building performance, and as such were implemented as full-scale architectural demonstrators.

Figure 1.6

Constructive re-conceptualisation: robotically built prototype based on a material-efficient construction typology developed by Friedrich Zollinger during the beginning of the twentieth century.

Gramazio Kohler Research, ETH Zürich, 2013

Assembly-driven design processes

WITHIN this research, the development of novel design methodologies is of particular importance. These must be informed by material, construction and fabrication criteria, and must be able to adapt to multiple functional requirements (Menges & Schwinn, 2012). This requires the development of new computational processes, which allow evaluation of the structural integrity of the final form and the evolving tolerances of the build-up process. As a basis for the realisation of all three demonstrators presented in this chapter a custom digital design and fabrication workflow has been developed and iteratively optimised (Figure 1.7). In this workflow, each timber element is defined as a logic entity including the specific information about its relation to neighbouring members from which to derive the end-cut information and the spatial sequencing of its robotic assembly.

At the same time, the design and fabrication workflow, which was embedded within a CAD platform, provided an interface to a structural analysis software for the evaluation of the structural integrity and performance of the design. This allowed for an intuitive design process of complex load-bearing timber assemblies by guaranteeing the breakdown of the form into an ideal number of components within a feasible spatial sequencing of the robotic assembly process. In addition to the geometry (length and end-cut angle) of the individual timber members, all the relevant

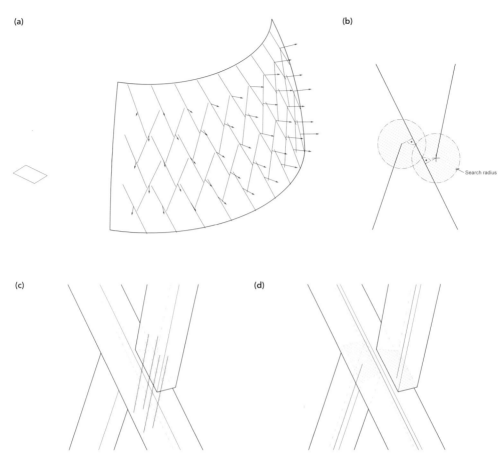

Figure 1.7

Workflow diagram of the digital design and fabrication process. From left to right: a) generation of wood member axis and definition of member orientation; b) definition of neighbouring components; c) generation of volumetric geometry, and d) generation of connection detailing.

Gramazio Kohler Research, ETH Zürich, 2012

fabrication related information, as for example the geometry of the predrilled holes for the joining and the path planning of the robotic arm, was integrated into a comprehensive and coherent data model. The ultimate goal of such a new (computational) design ontology is an architecture that is not defined primarily as a final geometric form, but as a complex and refined generative process of digital materialisation (Bonwetsch, Gramazio & Kohler, 2010).

Constructive systems

WHILE robotic technology enables the assembly of complex architectural structures from a large number of generic timber components, it raises the problem of how these components are best connected to each other. As such, advanced connection typologies, that are suitable for the implementation as a fully automated fabrication system, have to be developed, while taking maximal advantage of the possibilities of robotic fabrication by allowing for multiple degrees of geometric freedom (Willmann, Gramazio & Kohler, 2011).

A first approach to a constructive system accommodating these parameters has been identified in reciprocal frames structures. These supporting structures are interesting because of the simplicity and effectiveness of the reciprocally bearing elements (Figure 1.9). Based on a large number of timber members, which can be optimised according to the internal force flow of the structure, reciprocal frames structures are of particular interest in conjunction with digital fabrication techniques (Kohlhammer & Kotnik, 2011).

This connection typology has three fundamental advantages: First, by expanding the connection of three timber members at one single point in space into three separate eccentric connections between only two members, the components can be brought together once at a time, following a distinct assembly sequence which can be handled by a robotic arm. Second, as the individual members need only to be customised by an angled cut on both ends, this geometric adaptation can be carried out as an integrated step of the robotic process. And, third, the triangular arrangement of the node provides a simple means to control the stiffness of the connection by varying its geometric eccentricity and thus adapting it to specific fabrication and structural constraints of an automated assembly process.

Figure 1.8
Custom-developed reciprocal node connection for spatial robotic assemblies – by increasing or decreasing the size of its triangular arrangement, the stiffness of the connection can be individually adapted to specific local structural requirements.
Gramazio Kohler Research, ETH Zürich, 2012

Integrated robotic fabrication

IN this experimentation, all machining and assembly steps were integrated into a unified proto-typical fabrication process, where the single timber members are automatically gripped, cut at their ends, perforated and moved into their final position within one consistent workflow (Figure 1.10). The integration of all subsequent steps into one single process was fundamental in order to preserve digital information integrity and to avoid complex logistics such as the intermediate storage of prefabricated specific parts.

The issues of precision, as well as overall process and material tolerances, however, represent the main challenges. As a matter of fact, at this scale neither the anisotropic construction material, nor its robotic handling and positioning process are precise enough. In turn, tolerances in the build-up emerge, which, through their accumulation, cause major problems to the assembly process. This limitation requires the implementation of sensor-based feedback mechanisms, which allow the robots to register the actual geometry of the built structure in relation to the position of the timber member held by the robotic arm, and thereby to adjust the digital blueprint and

Figure 1.10

Non-standard robotic fabrication workflow, developed for the automated spatial assembly of discrete timber members. It features automated gripping and cutting, as well as robotic surface manipulation and spatial positioning.

Gramazio Kohler Research, ETH Zürich, 2013

Figure 1.11

Final full-scale demonstration object, based on the integrated robotic fabrication system using real-time sensor feedback. Key is to monitor the actual geometry of the individual timber members to automatically adjust the digital blueprint and the pre-computed motion path of the machine according to the factual material reality.

Bern University of Applied Sciences, 2014

the pre-computed motion path of the machine according to the factual material reality (Figure 1.11). At the same time, the real-time assessment of assembly tolerances during the build-up via a closed loop feedback system represents an important step towards the implementation of fully adaptive fabrication processes that are flexible and robust in their entirety. Here, the design of a particular assembly system is directly linked with the design of its fabrication process and the tools employed. Consequently, the infrastructural setup and material logistics heavily influence the robotic build-up, and hence its assembly performance.

Building-scale implementation

A SPECIFIC case for the industrial implementation of robotic timber construction is presented by 'The Sequential Roof' (Adam, 2014). Here, more than 48,624 timber slats are automatically assembled to form a 2,308 square metre large roof for the new building of the Institute for Technology in Architecture at ETH Zürich (see Figure 1.12). However, since the novel spatial connection typology had not yet been developed at the time of the project start in 2010, the project still relies on a layered construction system, radically extrapolating the initial 'The Sequentials' project series towards new building dimensions. In fact, it provides a first example for the realisation of automated large-scale timber assemblies, and particularly showcases a comprehensive end-to-end digital planning process, connecting design, structural analysis and construction.

As such, the design of the roof has been encapsulated in a custom computational parametric model, which was developed especially for this purpose (Figure 1.13); it is iteratively refined according to specific formal, constructive and structural criteria (e.g. slat sizes, maximisation of the overlaps between the timber members, optimisation of the nailing patterns of the connections, etc.)

as well as to parameters imposed by the automated robotic fabrication process (e.g. element manipulation, fabrication logics, etc.), and by the integration of embedded architectural subsystems, like sprinklers, lighting and openings. While the integration of all these diverse requirements left a very narrow solution space, which had to be algorithmically explored, this approach allowed for the computational optimisation of the design until the very last moment prior to the start of the physical fabrication process.

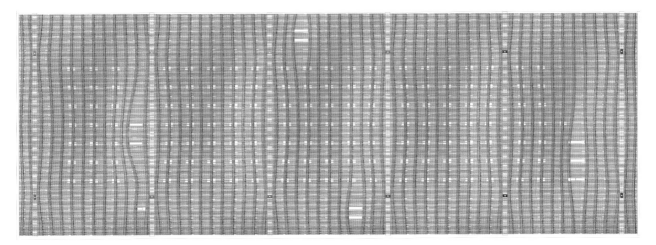

Figure 1.12
Top view of the 2,308 square meter large 'The Sequential Roof', consisting of 168 robotically prefabricated lattice trusses with a regular span of 14.70 meters to form a continuously graded constructive arrangement.
Arch-Tec-Lab AG, 2015

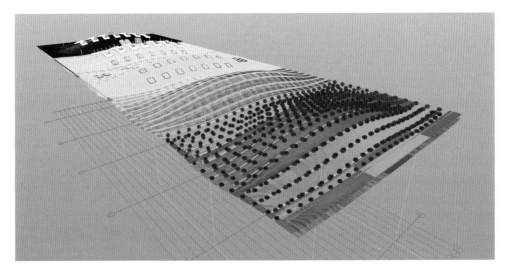

Figure 1.13
The design of the roof is encapsulated in a computational model, which was used for computationally generating the 'blueprint' of the structure, drawing on Python as programming language for the integration of the original architectural design in the CAD-environment.
Arch-Tec-Lab AG, 2015

Figure 1.14

Assembly of 'The Sequential Roof' of the Arch_Tec_Lab building of the Institute of Technology in Architecture (ITA), ETH Zürich. *Gramazio Kohler Research, ETH Zürich, 2015*

For the realisation of the roof, the contracted timber manufacturing company set up a new multi-functional robotic facility to enable the fully integrated manipulation and aggregation of components through constant digital guidance. As a consequence, the single working steps of each timber beam are fully integrated and automated, including for example an integrated quality monitoring by photographically checking for deviations or material errors.

Against this background, the combination of strong custom computational tools and flexible industrial fabrication logics of this first full-scale industrial implementation (Figure 1.14) illustrate the potential of robotic timber assembly processes. The performed tests have successfully demonstrated its feasibility and created knowledge that can be transferred to other explorations in the field of robotic timber construction.

Revitalised constructive nature

In conclusion, the vision of robotic timber construction, in which the integration of digital design and automated fabrication is at the centre of both the final object and also the process of its construction, radically expands the traditional spectrum of automated timber manufacturing and, simultaneously, introduces the use of robotic fabrication logics to this industrial sector. Therefore, the described explorations – spanning almost a decade of comprehensive research – pursue a radical shift in scale and scope, where non-standard timber structures can be efficiently aggregated from a multitude of single timber members to foster highly versatile timber constructions. Accordingly, this endeavour also promotes integrative computational design methodologies and techniques, where design decisions orchestrate a multitude of construction and fabrication attributes from the very beginning of the design process onward and up to the different stages of prototyping and final realisation. However, building-scale robotic timber construction is still in its infancy, and presents many challenges to the architecture and the timber sector. And yet this approach is captivating: It not only creates a new vision for future timber construction, but also emphasises new possibilities for the exploration of its real-world implementation – revitalising architecture's constructive nature and engaging with its own material roots.

References

Adam, H. (2014). Holzkonstruktionen, digital fabriziert. *Zuschnitt*, (53)20.

Bachmann, E., Egli, M., Zimmermann, F. & Fischer, R. (2008). Roboteranwendungen in der Holzwirtschaft. In *Best-Practice-Beispiele zur Roboteranwendung in der Holzwirtschaft* (2nd edn). Biel: Berner Fachhochschule. Architektur Holz und Bau.

Bonwetsch, T., Gramazio, F. & Kohler, M. (2010). Digitales Handwerk. In U. Hirschberg (ed.), *Grazer Architektur Magazin: Vol. 6. 2010. Nonstandard Structures* (1st edn, pp. 172–179). Vienna: Springer.

Gramazio, F. & Kohler, M. (2008). *Digital Materiality in Architecture*. Baden: Lars Müller Publishers.

Gramazio, F., Kohler, M. & Oesterle, S. (2010). Encoding Material. *Architectural Design*, 80(4), 108–115.

Kohlhammer, T. & Kotnik, T. (2011). Systemic Behaviour of Plane Reciprocal Frame Structures. *Structural Engineering International*, 21(1), 80–86.

Kuechle, H. & Volkmann, G. (1986). *WSI-Studie zur Wirtschafts- und Sozialforschung: Vol. 56. Holzwirtschaft im Wandel: Ökonomische und technologische Veränderungen in der Holzbearbeitung und Holzverarbeitung*. Cologne: Bund-Verlag.

Menges, A. & Schwinn, T. (2012). Manufacturing Reciprocities. In A. Menges (ed.), *Architectural Design*, 82(2), special issue, *Material Computation: Higher Integration in Morphogenetic Design*. London: Wiley.

Schindler, C. (2009). *Ein architektonisches Periodisierungsmodell anhand fertigungstechnischer Kriterien, dargestellt am Beispiel des Holzbaus*. PhD thesis, ETH Zürich (No. 18605).

Schwinn, T., Krieg, O. & Menges, A. (2012). Robotically Fabricated Wood Plate Morphologies: Robotic Prefabrication of a Biomimetic, Geometrically Differentiated Lightweight Finger Joint Timber Plate Structure. In S. Brell-Çokcan & J. Braumann (eds), *Rob/Arch 2012: Robotic Fabrication in Architecture, Art and Design* (pp. 48–61). Dordrecht: Springer.

Weinand, Y. & Buri, H.U. (2011). The Tectonics of Timber Architecture in the Digital Age. In H. Kaufmann and W. Nerdinger (eds), *Building with Timber: Paths into the Future* (pp. 56–63). Munich: Prestel.

Willmann, J., Gramazio, F. & Kohler, M. (2011). Die Operationalität von Daten und Material im Digitalen Zeitalter. In S. Hofmeister, C. Hellstern & S. Leitte (eds), *Detail Research. Positionen zur Zukunft des Bauens: Methoden, Ziele, Ausblicke* (1st edn, pp. 8–17). Munich: Detail Institut für Internationale Architektur-Dokumentation.

2

Additive robotic fabrication of complex timber structures

Volker Helm, Michael Knauss, Thomas Kohlhammer,
Fabio Gramazio, Matthias Kohler[1]
ETH Zürich, Gramazio Kohler Research, Switzerland

THE research into robotic timber assembly serves as a breeding ground for assembly- and material-aware construction methods that provide new opportunities for architecture and construction. In his contribution, Volker Helm, of the Gramazio Kohler Research group at ETH Zürich,[2] introduces the most recent investigations into innovative methods for robot-assisted assembly of complex timber structures. In cooperation with the Bern University of Applied Sciences[3] and within the framework of the Swiss National Research Programme 'Resource Wood' (NRP 66),[4] material-specific and constructive aspects of timber assembly are combined in a continuous digital design and manufacturing process taking advantage of both the flexibility of robotic manipulation and its capacity for precise spatial positioning. The project points the way towards future construction processes that are no longer encapsulated in a static plan, but rather are described by a programmed set of adaptive rules.

Spatially assembled constructions

THE current status of research in the area of digital fabrication of complex timber structures is limited mainly to the improvement in geometry and mechanical processing of components. This method involves high resource consumption because of material cutting procedures, like milling, as well as a high degree of manual labour. Especially in the case of a high geometric variability in construction, considerable costs must be taken into account.

Here, automatic assembly of generic timber components is an alternative that has been intensively investigated by the group of Gramazio Kohler Research at ETH Zürich and has already resulted in the first 1:1 construction prototypes, such as The Sequential Wall (Gramazio, Kohler & Oesterle, 2010). However, the two-dimensional stacking process considerably limits the

Figure 2.1
Prototype of a multi-layered truss system.
Bern University of Applied Sciences

performance and range of applications and the degree of geometrical freedom in the assembly of the components. Consequently, the research has extended to spatially assembled constructions, opening up new approaches for automatic manufacturing of architectural structures at full building-scale (Figure 2.1 and Figure 2.2).

The precise spatial positioning of wooden components represents the possibility of an innovative industrial procedure with a high degree of building precision, which can be manufactured without additional formwork or supports. In this context, the main goal was to create new combinations of fast-drying adhesive and automated assembly procedures, focusing on a multi-layered truss system as exemplary case. This approach made it possible to leave behind the standardised processing of wood and to design and manufacture new types of construction systems in a continuous digital process. The potential of such an integrally automated approach is still largely unexplored.

This interdisciplinary research approach requires a rigorous investigation of the individual working steps. Therefore the goal of the following chapter is to depict the different development and production steps of a full-scale multi-layered truss system. The following areas are examined

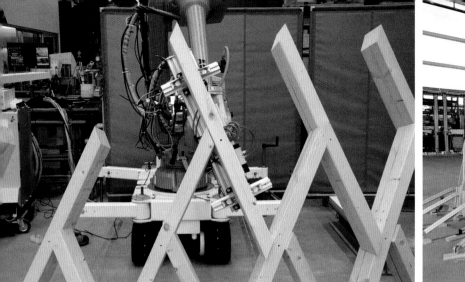

Figure 2.2

Prototype of a robotically fabricated Zollinger construction system applied to a double curved surface.
Gramazio Kohler Research, ETH Zürich

in detail: a) the constructive design system, b) fast-drying adhesives, c) automated fabrication and the consideration of the full scale prototype.

Constructive system

Tʜᴇ fundamental element of the constructive system is the expanded node. Here, a node in general is defined as a unit of contiguous bar-ends connected at or near one point within the system (Figures 2.3 and 2.4). Regarding fabrication and assembly of nodes, the complexity increases with the number of bars meeting at one point. The proposed geometric expansion of the node reduces the complexity and allows a simple sequential joining process. This, in turn, creates a node with structural reciprocity, which has bending resistance (Figure 2.3) and shear resistance (Figure 2.4), even though in its static system all connections are pin-jointed (Kohlhammer & Kotnik, 2011a).

Single layered structures with two-dimensional expanded nodes are well known, such as Reciprocal Frame Structures or the Zollinger-System. The flexural rigidity of these types is considerably low, as it depends on the cross-section of the bars (Kohlhammer, 2013).

This research focuses on multi-layered systems with three-dimensional nodes, as they promise a wider range of application than single layered systems because of a much higher bending resistance. This arises from their truss-like bearing capacity in addition to the reciprocal node behaviour. The developed system consists of three structural layers: 1) an upper layer, 2) a lower layer, and 3) an intermediate layer (Figure 2.5). In the upper and the lower layer, bars form a surface structure with reciprocal nodes. The intermediate layer consists of diagonal bars linking both outer layers.

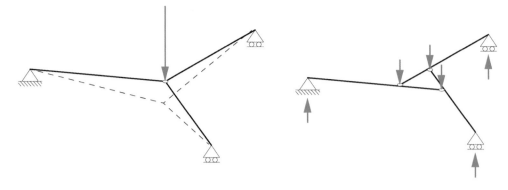

Figure 2.3

Load bearing behaviour perpendicular to plane: left: singular node, right: expanded node.

Gramazio Kohler Research, ETH Zürich

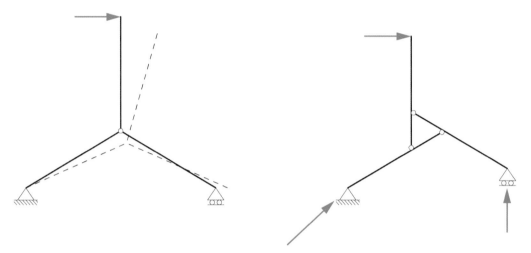

Figure 2.4

Load bearing behaviour in plane: left: singular node, right: expanded node.

Gramazio Kohler Research, ETH Zürich

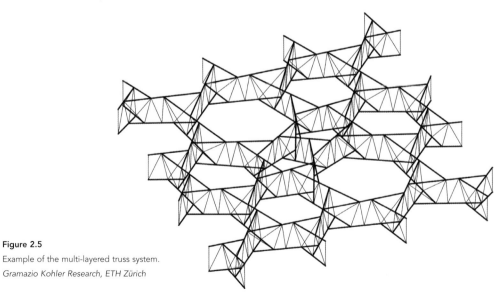

Figure 2.5

Example of the multi-layered truss system.

Gramazio Kohler Research, ETH Zürich

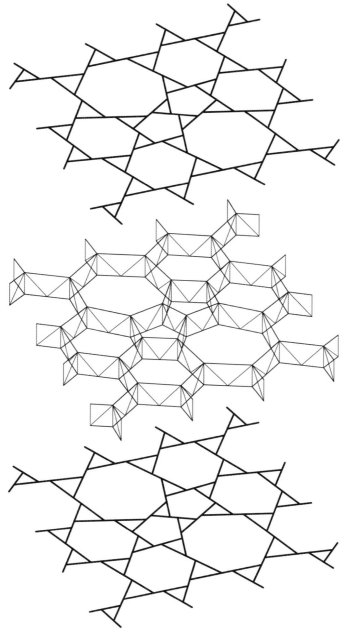

Figure 2.6
Partitioned structural behaviour of the system.
Gramazio Kohler Research, ETH Zürich

With respect to the vertical loads the structural behaviour of the system can be partitioned as follows (Figure 2.6).

1) Both outer layers act as a grid with reciprocal nodes. The grid has flexural rigidity, and thus the bars are under bending stress (Kohlhammer & Kotnik, 2011b).

2) The intermediate layer generates the structural behaviour of a truss grid, which induces normal forces in the bars.

The structural interest focuses on the interrelation of geometric parameters of the system and its static performance. The following parameters were defined as prime system-parameters, as they are seen as characteristics of this structural system: First the node expansion, which mainly influences the bearing capacity of the outer layers. Second, the slenderness of the structure (ratio of height and span), which only impacts the static performance of the trusses formed by the intermediate layer.

Parameter studies with a structural analysis software showed that the bearing capacity is primarily dependent upon the slenderness, and secondarily upon the node expansion. The importance of the respective parameters increases in accordance with the resistance of the joints, thus node expansion is more essential in the case of joints with lower bearing capacity.

Connection technology

GLUING is the main connection technology for this construction system because it can be fully integrated into a robotic fabrication process. However, standard adhesives for timber construction require both a long hardening time and substantial pressure during gluing, which, in fact, would not correspond to speedy construction enabled by a robotic arm. In order to overcome this barrier, cooperation with Nolax AG was established. Nolax AG is currently developing a fast-curing 2K PUR-Polyurea adhesive, which allows custom application processes. This near real-time curing adhesive (Brandmair et al., 2011) for non-structural connections (or low-force connections) may be extrapolated to fulfil the requirements found in high-performance timber construction.

This assumption was validated through a first feasibility study (Zock et al., 2014). It comprised of a comprehensive digital analysis, as well as the fabrication and testing of physical connection prototypes focusing on stiffness properties, tolerances and processing. All prototypes were designed as longitudinal joints connecting to the end-grain since this is the most critical connection. Two strategies were pursued: a) glue-only connections with low-load carrying capacity, using minimal expense in the manufacturing (Figure 2.7), and b) rod-shaped/flat elements glued with high load carrying capacity, and increased expenses for the automation (Figure 2.8).

Based on the results of the physical tests, glue-only connections were sufficient for this project. Therefore, the production of the final demonstrator (see following section) used glue-only connections without perforation to join the timber members.

Digital workflow and integrated automation

THE advantage in using digital information in the positioning of elements lies in the automated transmission and processing of data (Bachmann, 2005). With current timber construction techniques the digital process workflow typically ends with the manual fitting together of the

Figure 2.7

Test of glue-only connections: a) simply glued longitudinal joint without perforation; b) glued longitudinal joint with micro-perforation; c) glued longitudinal joint with 'impalements'; d) glued butting with micro-perforation.

Bern University of Applied Sciences

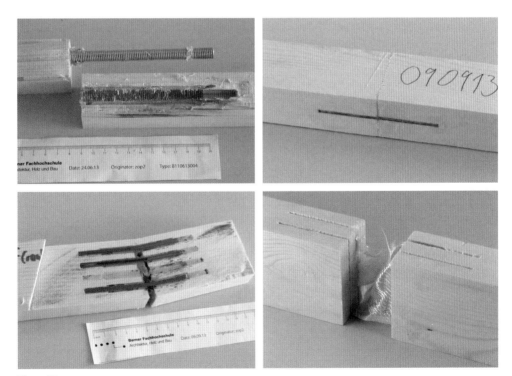

Figure 2.8

Rod-shaped/flat glued-in elements: a) glued-in threaded rod; b) glued-in perforated plate; c) glued-in carbon-fibre tubes; d) glued-in fibre glass fabric.

Bern University of Applied Sciences

Volker Helm, Michael Knauss, Thomas Kohlhammer, Fabio Gramazio, Matthias Kohler

parts. As a consequence, necessary assembly information is transmitted in an analogue way and processed by the worker (Bachmann, 2009). In contrast, a seamless digital workflow is required to assemble complex timber structures from a large number of individual components (Figure 2.9).

Accordingly, in the developed prototypical automation process all relevant fabrication data is gathered from a 3D-CAD model and written in an xml-structured file by an export tool. This file contains identification, length, cutting angles and target position of each timber member as well as the overall assembly order. The timber is cut with a mitre saw (Figure 2.10) that can be digitally controlled by an electric angle adjustment and conveying system. Its integration enables the adjustment of elements in real time, and sequences the timber elements for the robotic assembly process. The subsequent positioning was carried out by an industrial robot equipped with a pneumatic gripper. For the fabrication of the prototype, an industrial robot arm (Figure 2.11) was used, which is mounted on a linear axis to enlarge its working area. Within this setup, the demonstration prototype could be produced in seven segments, featuring a span length and width of 5m.

To connect two timber components, the robotic arm releases them at their target position. The length of the timber elements is calculated to leave a small interspace at the nodes. This interspace is then filled with the glue. A neoprene gasket (Figure 2.12) prevents leakage, ensuring injection pressure and defining the tolerance range at the same time. The gasket used can cover a gap of 5.0mm and can be compressed to 3.5mm. The adhesive is still injected manually with an applicator gun (Figure 2.13) to acquire comprehensive experience of the processing. The machine process of gluing will be automated once it is fully defined in future work.

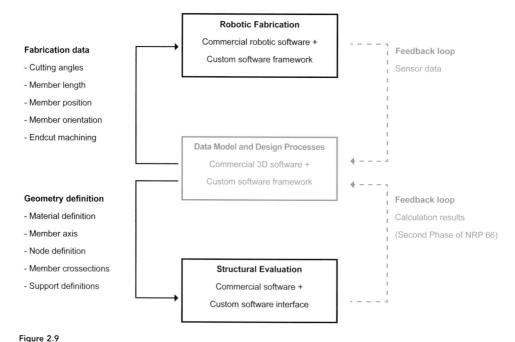

Figure 2.9

Diagram of the developed system components: left side, black or the digital design and fabrication workflow, and the functions which are currently under development; right side, blue or planned for the second phase of the project. *Gramazio Kohler Research, ETH Zürich.*

Figure 2.10

Automated timber cutting using a CNC mitre saw to specific length and end cut angles.

Bern University of Applied Sciences

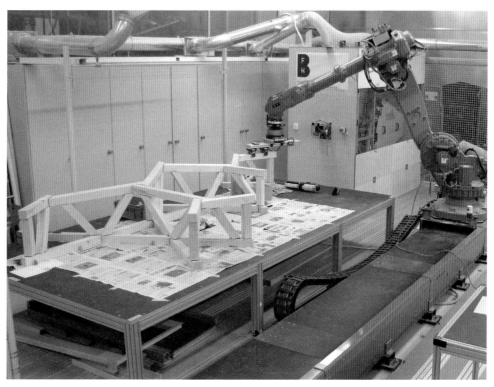

Figure 2.11

Robotic positioning in space.

Bern University of Applied Sciences

Figure 2.12

Neoprene seal for the T-joint connections.

Bern University of Applied Sciences

Figure 2.13

Glue injection with applicator gun.

Gramazio Kohler Research, ETH Zürich

Figure 2.14

The referencing process of a timber element.

Bern University of Applied Sciences

In the first steps, the segments were assembled to test the fabrication setup without any digital feedback (Helm et al., 2012). Precision for the glued connection was not achieved at this stage. To neutralise the aggregated tolerance, a custom scanning process was established to calculate the position of the timber elements just before their placement (Figure 2.14). With two measurements per axis, the orientation and actual position of the beam were determined. Dimensional deviations were calculated and the new target positioning is updated automatically. This referencing process reduced positioning errors to the required tolerance range which enabled the precise production of the final model.

Prototype of a multi-layered truss system

THE last step in this project phase was the implementation and structural check of the multi-layered truss prototype. The structure featured a span of 5.0 x 5.0m. The slenderness as one of the primary system parameters was set to seven, which results in a maximum height of 0.7m in the centre. In relation to the distribution of the bending moment, the height decreases to 0.5m towards the supports (Figure 2.15). The upper layer is flat to facilitate the use of the structure, e.g. as a floor slab. The height variability results in a curved lower layer. For the prototype all bars had cross-sections of 70 x 70mm.

To analyse the ultimate load of the prototype, a series of digital tests with structural analysis software were conducted. The calculated ultimate load on the level of design is 5.7 kN in addition to the dead loads. Resistances which refer to average values of tensile and shear tests of different qualities of spruce by EMPA (Eidgenössische Materialprüfungs- und Versuchsanstalt, 1955), result in an ultimate load of 14.2 kN in addition to the dead loads. As the developed system is redundant, the structure is still able to bear loads after breaking the connection with the highest stress at ultimate load level, simulating a crack. After the failure of the first critical node (I) (Figure 2.15), the ultimate load of the structure decreases to 70%. After another failure at the second critical node (II), the remaining bearing capacity is 66%.

In order to understand the behaviour of a structure with glue-only connections, a first initial large-scale loading test was performed. During the test eight central nodes were vertically loaded with sand. Within this testing procedure, it was not possible to reach the point of failure. The test had to be stopped at a load level of 20 kN. One interpretation of this result could be the outstanding quality of the wood used for the prototype. Another explanation could be that the redundancy of the system implies an extraordinary bearing capacity due to changes in load distribution.

To finally test the structure to its maximal load, a test setup was implemented by using six hydraulic cylinders and a test rig (Figure 2.16). However, the second loading of the structure resulted in a much lower load of only 8.5 kN. It is possible that the high load during the first test already weakened some of the connections. The experience clearly shows that timber elements which have been previously highly loaded often fail in retesting at much lower loads compared to the first loading.

As a conclusion of the first physical test, the ultimate load is at least 350% higher than the result of the calculation. Furthermore, the second test showed the same mode of collapse as in the digital simulations. This means that the consequence of the first connection failure does not include the total collapse of the structure, but a residual bearing capacity of about 70%. The second load test also confirmed the sequence of critical nodes as predicted from the computational simulations. For a detailed confirmation of the calculation model, a series of physical tests are necessary.

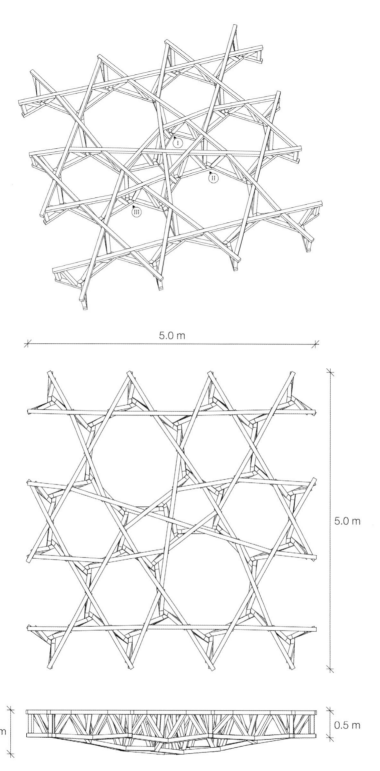

5.0 m

5.0 m

0.7 m   0.5 m

Figure 2.15

Perspective, top view and elevation of the prototype.

Gramazio Kohler Research, ETH Zürich

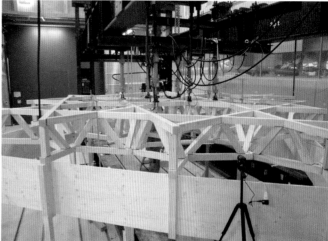

Figure 2.16
1:1 test setup of the final prototype object.
Bern University of Applied Sciences

Future work

OUR goal is to further advance the developed techniques and methods for robot-based timber construction. In addition to the further refinement of the experimental setup, including, for example, enhanced robotic control and automated design generation of construction scenarios, we will continue to explore the integration of material-driven feedback processes in the robot-based assembly. By so linking the formal, constructive and fabrication parameters, an optimisation of the entire generation process can be achieved. Here it becomes apparent that with a certain 'critical mass' of complexity, construction components with mutual dependencies, the use of digital design, and fabrication processes becomes not only meaningful but mandatory. Correspondingly, the computational design can no longer be encapsulated in a static plan. Rather it is described by a programmed set of rules which advantageously allow for seamless adaptations, throughout and even at very late stages of the design process. The intent is thus less a purely functional modus operandi of digital fabrication than a focus on equally assembly-driven and material-aware construction methods, fostering robotic timber assembly as a unique breeding ground to induce new opportunities in architecture (Gramazio, Kohler & Wilmmann, 2014).

Acknowledgements

THIS project was supported within the framework of the Swiss National Science Foundation NRP 66 'Resource Wood' research programme and resulted from the cooperation between Gramazio Kohler Research at ETH Zürich and the Bern University of Applied Sciences. The authors thank Nolax AG (industrial partner) for their support as well as all collaborators from ETH Zürich and Bern University of Applied Sciences. The authors are also grateful for the generous support of Dr Jan Willmann. Special thanks goes to Luka Piškorec and the students of the elective course Complex Timber Structures in 2013 (Marisa Brunner, Christian Grewe Rellmann, Rossitza Kotelova, Enrique Ruiz Durazo, Andreas Thoma).

References

Bachmann, E. (2005). *Robotereinsatz in der Produktion – Eine Chance für den Holzbau*. Conference Bayern Innovativ. Rosenheim.

Bachmann E. (2009). *Optimierungspotenzial Vorfertigung*. Conference Top Programm Holz. Dottikon.

Brandmair, A., Dobmann, A., Meyer, S., Schwotzer, W. & Steiner, P. (2011). Ultraschnelle Montagetechnik. *Adhäsion Kleben & Dichten*, 55(12), 22–25.

Eidgenössische Materialprüfungs- und Versuchsanstalt (1955). Über den Einfluss von Wassergehalt, Raumgewicht, Faserstellung und Jahresringe auf die Festigkeit und Verformbarkeit schweizerischen Fichten-, Tannen-, Lärchen-, *Rotbuchen- und Eichenholzes*. EMPA Bericht Nr. 183. Zurich.

Gramazio, F., Kohler, M. & Oesterle, S. (2010). Encoding Material. *Architectural Design*, 80(4), 108–115.

Gramazio, F., Kohler, M. & Willmann, J. (2014). *The Robotic Touch: How Robots Change Architecture*. Zurich: Park Books.

Helm, V., Ercan, S., Gramazio, F. & Kohler, M. (2012). In-Situ Robotic Construction: Extending the Digital Fabrication Chain in Architecture. In J.K. Johnson, M. Cabrinha & K. Steinfeld (eds), *ACADIA 2012 Synthetic Digital Ecologies: Proceedings of the 32nd annual conference of the Association for Computer Aided Design in Architecture, ACADIA* (pp. 169–176). San Francisco: ACADIA.

Kohlhammer, T. (2013). *Strukturoptimierung von stabförmigen Flächentragwerken mittels reziproker Analyse*. PhD Thesis, ETH Zürich (No. 21565).

Kohlhammer, T. & Kotnik, T. (2011a). Discrete Analysis: A Method to Determine the Internal Forces of Lattice Structures. In *Proceedings of the 35th IABSE-IASS Symposium: Taller, Longer, Lighter*. London.

Kohlhammer, T. & Kotnik, T. (2011b). Systemic Behaviour of Plane Reciprocal Frame Structures. *Structural Engineering International*, 21(1), 80–86.

Zock, P., Bachmann, E., Gramazio, F., Kohler, M., Kohlhammer T., Knauss, M., Sigrist, C. & Sitzmann, S. (2014). Additive robotergestützte Herstellung komplexer Holzstrukturen. In *46. Tagungsband Fortbildungskurs Holzverbindungen mit Klebstoffen für die Bauanwendung*. Swiss Wood Innovation Network (S-WIN) (pp. 197–208). Weinfelden.

Notes

1. The complete list of the authors, including the project partners from Bern University of Applied Sciences, Department of Architecture, Wood and Civil Engineering, Switzerland, are as follows: Volker Helm, Michael Knauss, Thomas Kohlhammer, Fabio Gramazio, Matthias Kohler, Stefan Sitzmann, Peter Zock, Eduard Bachmann, Christophe Sigrist.
2. ETH Zürich, Chair of Architecture and Digital Fabrication, Switzerland, http://gramazio-kohler.arch.ethz.ch/ (27.02.2015)
3. Bern University of Applied Science, Department of Architecture, Wood and Civil Engineering, Switzerland, http://www.bfh.ch/en/bfh/the_six_departments/architecture_wood_and_civil_engineering.html (27.02.2015)
4. National Research Programme NRP 66 – Resource Wood, http://www.nrp66.ch/en (27.02.2015)

3

The Sequential Roof

Aleksandra Anna Apolinarska, Michael Knauss,
Fabio Gramazio, Matthias Kohler
ETH Zürich, Gramazio Kohler Research, Switzerland

COMPUTATIONAL design provides the opportunity to integrate all planning disciplines and stakeholders of wood architecture from the earliest planning stages and, by consequence, to span across the statutory design, fabrication, and construction phases. Aleksandra Anna Apolinarska of Gramazio Kohler Research at ETH Zürich, introduces research related to the Arch_Tec_Lab building's roof structure, an industry transfer project in robotic fabrication of complex timber structures. In her contribution, she presents the specific design features, the non-standard concurrent development process and the unprecedented fabrication and assembly method, all of which showcase how innovative computational design and manufacturing processes not only change the logistics of timber construction but also can give rise to novel architectural solutions.

Project description

Introduction

THE Arch_Tec_Lab building project (Figure 3.1) was launched at the Institute of Technology in Architecture (ITA) of ETH Zürich in 2009 as a multi-disciplinary endeavour to design the institute's new laboratory and office building located on the Hönggerberg campus in Zurich.[1] The building will house a state-of-the-art robotic laboratory, workshops, offices and studio spaces, and is conceived as a realscale demonstrator showcasing innovative approaches to architecture and construction in terms of parametric design, digital fabrication, sustainability, HVAC (heating, ventilation and air conditioning), MEP (mechanical, electrical and plumbing) and structural systems.

One of the key features of the project is the robotically fabricated timber roof, designed and developed by the Gramazio Kohler Research group at ETH Zürich in tight collaboration with the planning team of the building.[2] The group stands at the forefront of research in robotic

Figure 3.1
Finished construction of the Arch_Tec_Lab building looking towards the office spaces.
Gramazio Kohler Research, ETH Zürich

fabrication in architecture, and their long-term investigation of robotic assembly of timber structures (Gramazio & Kohler, 2008) is crowned by the realisation of the full-scale construction project
presented here (Gramazio, Kohler & Willmann, 2014).

Roof design

Covering a total area of 2,300 square metres, the free-form structure consists of nearly 50,000
unique timber elements, designed using bespoke algorithms and fabricated and assembled with
robotic machinery (Figure 3.2). Hovering above a double-height open office space, 28 metres
wide and 80 metres long, the whole roof rests upon 12 prominent steel columns, unobstructed
by partition walls. The seemingly continuous, undulating surface consists in fact of 168 trusses,
with a regular span of 14.7 metres and 1.15 metres width. Each truss is made of 23 layers of 50mm
thick timber slats stacked together in an alternating manner. The layering logic is derived from a
basic form of a truss consisting of continuous top and bottom chords with diagonal webs and is
adapted according to the layering concept. For the chords to be continuous, the top and bottom
slats are arranged into three-layer chain-like packages, as opposed to diagonal members which can
be accommodated in one layer (Figure 3.3).

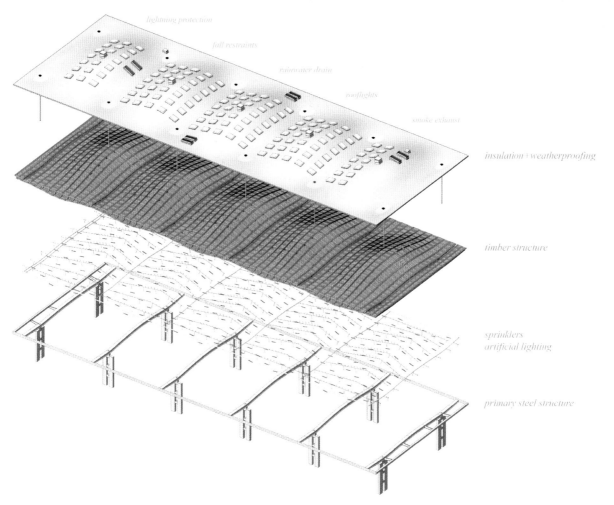

lightning protection

fall restraints

rainwater drain

rooflights

smoke exhaust

insulation \ weatherproofing

timber structure

sprinklers
artificial lighting

primary steel structure

Figure 3.2
Overview of the roof build-up. Roofing layers, skylights, smoke exhaust, sprinklers, lighting and other systems are tightly integrated into the roof structure.

This topological configuration exhibits great flexibility and allows for ample variance of truss shapes. For example, the curvature of the top and bottom chord, segment lengths and the structural height can be adapted to fit local or global needs (Figure 3.4). The distribution of the diagonal webs and connection nodes within the truss can be adjusted to improve structural performance or to adapt to interfaces with other building parts. For instance, the node distances can be locally increased to allow for the oblong smoke exhaust shafts to pass through the roof. Also, due to the redundancy within the structure, individual elements may be left out to create a recess where needed.

The spatial density of the trusses enables seamless integration of the structure with various subsystems. On the outside, they form a continuous surface onto which weatherproofing layers can be directly installed, without the need of secondary boarding. This is a major benefit, as covering a double-curved surface with panels would require considerable effort. From the inside, the lower

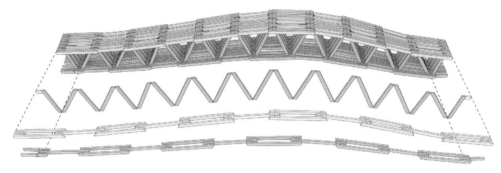

Figure 3.3

Layering logic of the trusses. Between every three chord elements (grey) there is a layer of web elements (blue). Together the truss consists of 23 layers of 50mm timber slats.

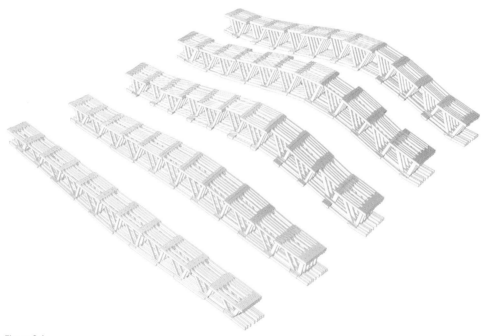

Figure 3.4

Form variance of the timber trusses. In general, neither any two beams nor any two timber slats are identical. All timber slats are cut at their unique angles and lengths ranging from 0.13 to 3.17 metres.

chord layer creates a tectonically vivid ceiling with porosity favourable for interior acoustics, as well as space and support for subsystems like artificial lighting, sprinklers, electrical cable routes and other devices (Figure 3.2). Conversely, the structure is transparent enough for the daylight coming from the skylights to permeate through, which has been evaluated experimentally in scale model tests using an artificial sky dome (Adam, 2014).

Timber

Iᴺ the context of growing awareness over the use of natural resources, it was one of the project's objectives to use simple and possibly low-engineered timber products, such as solid structural timber of strength class C24. The choice fell on 50mm thick, two-layer glued softwood, with planks cut on a split-heart basis to guarantee higher form stability and to reduce the risk of fibre splitting due to nailing. For the sake of material efficiency, three different cross-section heights were used: 115mm, 140mm and 180mm. The material was produced in the form of 10-metre long finger-joined, untreated, planed slats, with a reduced moisture content of around 10%. Compared to simple solid structural wood, this assures fewer moisture-related shape changes like bending and warping, which is essential to keep all connections in a layered structure gap-free. Natural behaviours like shrinking and swelling of timber were carefully taken into account in the planning process. To accommodate the changes in the direction perpendicular to the grain (which accumulate across all the 23 layers), a 15mm gap was introduced between the trusses.

Joints

Tᴏ achieve a fully automated manufacturing process, only connection techniques that could be fully automated were considered. One of them was gluing with one-component polyurethane adhesive, which cures by binding moisture contained in wood, and which is widely employed in the timber industry. It requires, however, a certain contact pressure which might be difficult to achieve and control when pressing on a skewed stack of slats.

A competitive technique was a mechanical connection using nails. One of its advantages is its ductile character: the nails deform and bend before the brittle failure of wood occurs, which means that the structural collapse is not abrupt and allows for smoother re-distribution of stresses. Compared to the glued option, however, it poses additional geometric challenges. Nails can cause a fibrous material such as timber to split along the grain, and preserving minimal intervals between nails and distances to the element's edges is necessary to reduce this risk. As specified in the Swiss norms (SIA 265:2003), these distances depend on the shank diameter of the nail and grain direction of wood. This can be interpreted as an elliptical zone around a nail's centre which must be kept clear (Figure 3.5). For the nails with 3.4mm shank diameter used in this project, this distance amounts to 34mm in the grain direction and 17mm in the direction perpendicular to the grain. As each nail connects two pieces of wood, it must not only take the positions of other nails in the layer below into account, but also the orientation of the ellipse according to the grain direction of each layer. The minimal distance to the element's edge, 51mm and 20.4mm respectively, is also grain-dependant, which means that the permitted zone between two overlapping timber elements is eccentric to the axis lines of both elements. Moreover, the permitted zone varies depending on the actual geometry of each two overlapping slats and their relative position to each other. On top of that, the required number of nails (ranging between four and 20) is determined by structural calculations for each of the 94,380 connections individually (Figure 3.6).

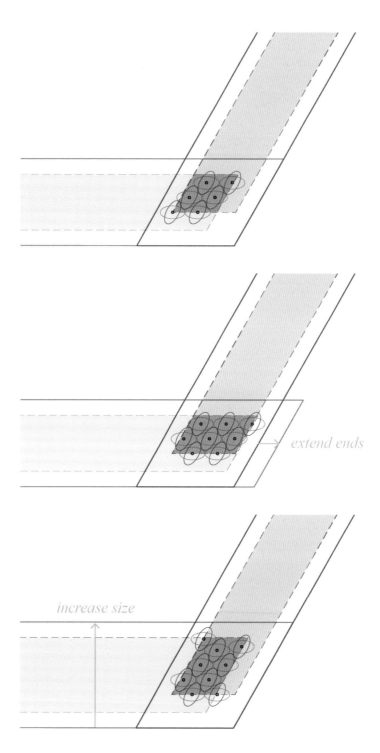

extend ends

increase size

Figure 3.5

Connection between two timber elements: a) permitted overlap areas and possible nail distribution. Increasing the overlap area is possible by b) extending slat ends or c) increasing the cross-section height.

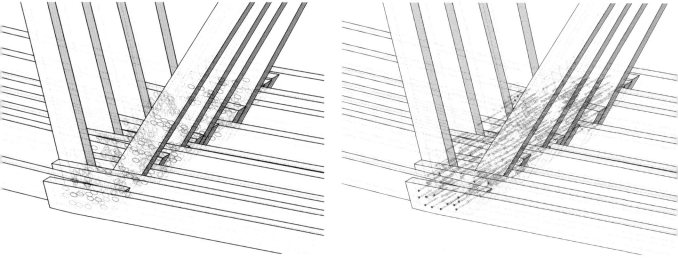

Figure 3.6
Distribution of nails through all 23 layers, according to geometry constraints and nail numbers in each layer, results in a highly complex nail pattern.

Design and construction process

Design framework

Tʜɪs multidisciplinary and highly experimental project required collaborative involvement from all parties and planners from a very early stage, including structural engineers, consultants for timber construction, fire safety, weatherproofing and day lighting, as well as potential industry partners. Going beyond the established statutory design phases, concept development, structural analysis and fabrication details were developed concurrently. To achieve this, from an architect's perspective, different types of input information needed to be linked and processed within one integrated design framework. Apart from the usual coordination between disciplines, it enforced an exchange of large amounts of data from different sources (for example structural analysis) and active negotiation of the tightly interrelated architectural, structural and fabrication parameters within one computational model in an iterative development process. In the absence of suitable off-the-shelf solutions, several bespoke pieces of software were written as add-ons to commercially available NURBS-based[3] 3D-modelling and structural analysis software packages. One of the algorithms, for example, generated the geometrically intricate model of the structure, its volumetric representation and an abstracted data model for the structural analysis software and fabrication simulation. Another procedure automated the setup of structural calculations based on this data model.[4] The results of the structural analysis (such as the number of nails needed for each connection) were further processed by the fabrication simulation algorithm which also generated the nailing pattern.[5] An initial roof model, consisting of equally sized members with a cross-section of 50 x 100mm, proved to be far from fulfilling all structural and fabrication

Aleksandra Anna Apolinarska, Michael Knauss, Fabio Gramazio, Matthias Kohler

requirements. To resolve this, the design was refined iteratively by locally modifying the geometry of individual elements (Figure 3.7). If excessive internal forces (buckling, shear or normal stresses) indicated the need for a larger cross-section of a certain element, or if the nail pattern failed to accommodate all the nails required in a joint (for instance due to an insufficient overlap area between two slats), the geometry of an individual element or a pair of elements was modified by extending slat ends or increasing their cross-section. After several iterations, as soon as all structural and fabrication issues were cleared, the design was immediately ready for production with no need for further post-processing, as all details, dimensions, calculations and manufacturing data had already been generated in the process (Figure 3.8).

Structural analysis and tests

As this kind of connection and structural arrangement is not explicitly described by regulations, and as there are no established calculation models for structural analysis of such a structure, the calculations needed to be validated by means of physical experiments. First, a series of specimens consisting of a single node made of three slats were tested in various geometrical

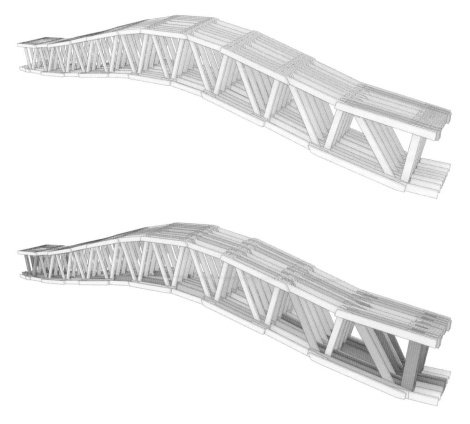

Figure 3.7

Iterative design development and dimensioning. a) Initial model with minimal slat sizes; b) model after the last iteration with locally modified elements' dimensions, fulfilling all structural and fabrication requirements.

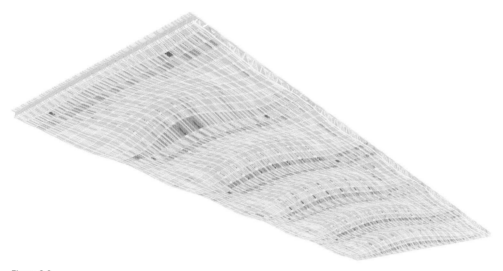

Figure 3.8
Final model of the complete roof structure. The computational design tools allowed the handling of the complexity and the differentiation of the aggregation of the material by dimensioning the members individually.

Figure 3.9
Validation of structural calculations. a) stress test of a single node with elements at 45° angle; b) stress test of a complete full-scale truss.

configurations, including different angles between slats (0°, 45° and 90°) and different nail patterns (with uniform, asymmetric or eccentric distribution) (Figure 3.9a). The data received from the results was used to refine the calculation model that was employed in further design development, dimensioning and detailing. The final design was validated by load testing of 15 full-scale trusses as control samples (Figure 3.9b). At the same time, the trusses produced for the tests served as prototypes for the newly developed manufacturing process.

Aleksandra Anna Apolinarska, Michael Knauss, Fabio Gramazio, Matthias Kohler

Robotic fabrication

INTEGRATING cutting-edge robotic fabrication methods with advanced computational design techniques opens up new opportunities for formal expression as well as construction methods (Gramazio, Kohler & Oesterle, 2010). In this project, the design concept and the construction process were developed simultaneously from the very beginning, which is a novel approach. The use of digitally controlled fabrication tools enabled the design of a structure of a high geometrical complexity, liberated from constraints of standardisation and repetition. Moreover, the fully automated robotic assembly (with no manual labour involved) facilitated the use of small elements and simple, generic and notch-free joints. Conversely, the bespoke digital fabrication setup was developed simultaneously with the design. Not only the layering logic of the trusses reflects the construction sequence and manufacturing constraints, but also the number of possible different slat sizes was derived from an optimum between maximal operational space of the facility, minimal time losses for material feeding during production, and, conversely, a minimal number of cross-sections approximating ideal dimensions from a structural point of view.

The fabrication setup, proactively developed by the contractor for this challenging project, consisted of a six-axis gantry robot with a mechanical wrist and exchangeable end-effectors, a sawing table, a tool changing rack and a repository of 10m-long timber slats in the three different sizes (Figure 3.10). The trusses were built layer by layer using the following steps. 1) First, the material is picked by the gripper and cut by an automatically adjustable saw at the defined length and angles. 2) Then, the piece is placed in the target position and fixed preliminarily with one nail at each end. This allows to precisely control and correct its position at each end. Subsequently, the remaining nails are shot. 3) In some cases, additional trimming is needed in situ after the slat is fixed. For this step, the gripper end-effector is exchanged for a circular saw. 4) Finally, before the next layer is built, every node is automatically documented and checked for deviations or errors by a photographic camera attached to the machine.

The fundamental feature of this manufacturing concept is that the fabrication of parts and assembly take place simultaneously. Each timber element is cut to size only shortly before being joined with the rest of the truss – hence reducing logistics to a minimum by avoiding the need of labelling the elements, as each piece is installed in the right place straight away.

Figure 3.10 (facing page)

Custom six-axis overhead gantry robot of ERNE AG Holzbau, featuring a translational axis with a mechanical wrist and three additional rotational axes to perform fully automated fabrication tasks within an effective workspace of 48 x 6.1 x 1.9m. The control software enabling the fabrication was developed by ROB Technologies AG (Arch_Tec_Lab, 2015).

Aleksandra Anna Apolinarska, Michael Knauss, Fabio Gramazio, Matthias Kohler

Summary

THE timber trusses were fabricated and brought on site in 2015. The Arch_Tec_Lab building was opened to students and researchers in summer 2016. But already before it was finished, the project demonstrated how integrating advanced computational design tools, material-aware detailing and fabrication-driven concept development can lead to novel design and construction methods.

As a pioneering endeavour, the project presented certain challenges and risks to planners and contractors, and ultimately the client (ETH Zürich). It required novel design tools, custom calculation models for structural analysis, validation by means of physical load tests, and bespoke and fully automated fabrication processes. The successful development and realisation of the project was only feasible by involvement and integration of all planning disciplines and stakeholders from the earliest stages and, by doing so, going beyond the statutory design and construction phases.

Acknowledgements

THE authors would like to thank the collaboration partners of 'The Sequential Roof' project for giving the opportunity of realising such an experiment and their generous support in the overall project. This includes the following realisation and consulting partners: Overall planning: Arch-Tec-Lab AG (Guido Züger); structural engineering: Dr. Lüchinger+Meyer Bauingenieure AG; timber engineering: SJB Kempter Fitze AG (Franz Tschümperlin); manufacturing and realisation: ERNE AG Holzbau; digital integration and fabrication control: ROB Technologies AG (Dr Tobias Bonwetsch, Dr Ralph Bärtschi); structural design consultancy: Prof. Dr Josef Schwartz (ETH Zürich); timber structure engineering consultancy: Prof. Dr Andrea Frangi (ETH Zürich). Much of 'The Sequential Roof' project would have not been possible without the valuable support of the Institute of Technology in Architecture (ITA) and ETH Zürich, which initiated and supported this exciting endeavour.

References

Adam, H. (2014). Holzkonstruktionen, digital fabriziert. *Zuschnitt*, (53), 20–21.

Gramazio, F. & Kohler, M. (2008). *Digital Materiality in Architecture: Gramazio & Kohler*. Baden: Müller.

Gramazio, F., Kohler, M. & Oesterle, S. (2010). Encoding Material. *Architectural Design*, 80(4), 108–115.

Gramazio, F., Kohler, M. & Willmann, J. (2014). *The Robotic Touch: How Robots Change Architecture*. Zurich: Park Books.

Swiss norm SIA 265:2003 *Timber Structures* (SN 505265), Chapter 6.4.

Notes

1.   http://ita.arch.ethz.ch/index.php/en/arch-tec-lab (Accessed 31 August 2015).

2.   http://gramaziokohler.arch.ethz.ch/web/d/forschung/201.html (Accessed 31 August 2015).

3.   Non-uniform rational basis spline.

4.   Structural model and calculations as well as the interface with the structural analysis software set up and conducted by the civil engineering firm Dr. Lüchinger+Meyer Bauingenieure AG, Zurich.

5.   Given that every connection is potentially a unique situation, no regular grid can efficiently distribute all of the 815,984 nails. ROB Technologies AG from Zurich developed a bespoke algorithmic method for generating the nail pattern.

PART TWO

IBOIS Laboratory for Timber Construction, EPFL, Switzerland

4

Timber fabric structures
Innovative wood construction

Yves Weinand

IBOIS Laboratory for Timber Constructions, EPFL, Switzerland

Fʟᴇxɪʙɪʟɪᴛʏ and softness, attributes associated with textiles and fabrics, seem at first glance anathema to robust and static load-bearing structures of the built environment. Yves Weinand, director of IBOIS, the Laboratory for Timber Constructions at the École Polytechnique Fédérale de Lausanne, not only highlights the need for reconsidering established notions of timber structures in the light of the environmental challenges that the building industry is facing, but also proposes an entirely new category of timber structures that can be conceived as Timber Fabric structures on the building scale. Beyond a mere 'textile' analogy, he argues for a true understanding and analysis of textile principles of wood on a micro and macro scale. First prototypical results of the development of these structures are presented in this chapter, providing the conceptual framework for the development of novel approaches and methods for the design, simulation, analysis and digital fabrication of Timber Fabric structures in architecture.

Introduction

Oᴠᴇʀ the last two centuries, the predomination first of steel, then of reinforced concrete within research and application in the field of civil engineering and material science has left a gap in timber research from a structural point of view. The intuitive knowledge of the engineers' predecessors as well as that of the carpenters during the eighteenth century has been lost with the rise of the 'Ingénieur des Ponts et Chaussées', who has not taken advantage of timber as a construction material, having a priori accorded it a lower level of importance than steel and concrete. However, the environmental arguments for enlarging the possible uses of renewable timber resources are increasingly self-evident. Society's burgeoning awareness of the urgent need to identify sustainable building materials has become an important influence in timber construction's renewed economic importance in recent years. Environmental considerations are helping to restore or establish the legitimate use of timber in our cities' constructions on a scale unprecedented since many centuries.

Timber construction demands interdisciplinary approaches, involving architecture, civil engineering and material science. It is only when examined more closely than traditionally in the construction industry that timber reveals its surprisingly strong connections to textiles and its vast potential for the application of textile techniques. Timber can be classified as both a soft and a viscous material, having smooth properties and being subject to creep. Wood is composed of a multitude of cellulose fibres, which through their flexibility allow elastic bending and high curvature. Such properties suggest that building-scale woven flexible timber structures could offer exceptional performance in resisting seismic instability, as well as extreme wind or snow loads (Figure 4.1). To date, the potential for building-scale woven structures to significantly reduce the risk of structural collapse in the face of such challenges has not been systematically explored. Truly interdisciplinary research approaches linking architecture with civil engineering remain uncommon.

The research subject 'timber fabric' is in itself an act of invention, since civil engineering structures typically rely on robust elements (such as beams and columns) as constituent parts of a bigger integral unit in order to achieve load-bearing qualities.

Society does not presently associate major civil engineering infrastructure and equipment with expressions like 'textile' or 'timber'. For most people, 'textile' has a connotation of softness, which seems incompatible with the general context of engineering structures. Although, 'textile' has a large range of applications and interpretations, to date there have been no attempts to employ its qualities and production technologies at the scale of timber construction. Yet the strategy of devising textile-like (woven) timber surfaces can exploit wood's fibrous, inherently flexible nature and turn a characteristic that until now was perceived as a limitation of the raw material, into a structural advantage. The invention of structural timber fabric embodies both a vision of the future and an understanding of the past. It is inspired by the understanding of building as an integrated planning process, where craft, technique, aesthetics and structural engineering aspects converge, like they did just before the revolutionary 'Age of Industrialisation', but this time using contemporary engineering methods and tools.

A new generation of timber derived structures is also an act of creativity within the field of architecture and specific contemporary architectural approaches. The raw resource in question has innate qualities (such as smoothness) that can also satisfy aesthetic and conceptual qualities that architects value. The emerging tools in digital architecture and design software seen as an instrument to conceive architecture have opened the way for broader applications of digital technology, including those of a technical nature. Because of technical advances, the integration of textile principles, technologies and fabrication systems is now feasible in ways that were unthinkable only a few years ago.

The presented research reveals that techniques such as friction-welding, knitting, weaving and even origami can be applied to timber on a building scale. The work of IBOIS is already demonstrating that the application of such techniques can radically expand timber's range of technical and aesthetic attributes. Such techniques allow the invention of timber products fit for novel purposes at a time when society is both culturally and economically ready to accept timber as a construction material. Significant advantages of such techniques can be foreseen, as they facilitate

Figure 4.1
Timber fabric experimental woven wood structure.

the creation of large-scale free-form structures from small repeating units (Figure 4.2); this opens the way to an expansion of the uses of both timber off-cuts and post-consumer recycled wood products as high-quality construction material.

The capacity to impose curvature in building parts (such as glue-laminated timber beams) has until now not opened up a broader exploration of what this technique can lead to. However, the implications are profound. Timber has the dual capacity to be formed and to retain an imposed form; the use of textile principles allows us to take advantage of these capacities in order to produce durable, curved timber elements (Figure 4.3). Timber is now becoming amenable to the realisation of highly complex woven structural systems where an important number of interactions of pieces of relatively small size constitute robust large-scale structures. These fulfil necessary production efficiency and safety considerations, combining aesthetic qualities such as lightness and light transmission with functional qualities such as a desired degree of rigidity or flexibility. The old-fashioned image of the 'chalet' and related vernacular architecture will be replaced by a contemporary interpretation; the presented research helps establish timber as a modern, high-tech material that can play a central role in a society concerned with sustainability.

The combination of the IBOIS research ingredients, namely timber, textile, fabric and civil engineering structures, enable the development of free-form structures without precedent. This area of research could also lead to new forms in furniture making, carpentry, and design in general. Furthermore, it could have implications for other timber related applications, such as floor finishing and separating walls. Even if at this point in time many of the specific applications remain pure conjecture, the interdependent design and physical conception of hitherto inexistent forms of woven timber constructions can only stimulate further developments of the timber industries and the use of timber in the construction sector.

On a broader level, the investigations of the IBOIS Group contribute to a more profound understanding of spatial structures in general, and set new precedents for cooperative interaction between the architects and engineers who will analyse those structures.

Figure 4.2

Composite box trusses made from curved folded wood panels.

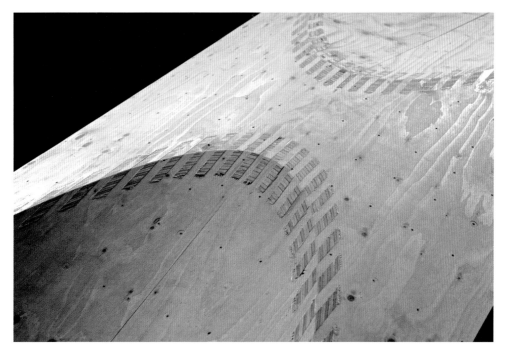

Figure 4.3
Prototype of the Curved Folded Wood Pavilion.

Potential impacts

Promoting a renewable material by appealing design

WITH the contemporary discussion about global climate change in mind, it is clear that there is a need to change traditional methods of building. Alternative energy resources need to be made accessible, and a lower consumption of energy needs to be achieved. Here the production and energy consumption of building structures plays an important role, which makes timber, a renewable resource, a promising building material that should be used more frequently. However, in order to persuade investment in environmentally friendly materials like timber, the products must be more attractive. In the past, sustainable architecture using timber often had a rustic, primitive and alternative touch, which, though attractive to some, was repellent to many other potential clients. In order to access the latter group, design needs to be treated as a serious criterion. The design of contemporary and appealing architecture with timber is both feasible and necessary if it is to become more widely used in construction.

Buildings with a higher disaster resistance

TRADITIONAL design and development strategies of structures are largely based on the concepts of stiffness and efficiency. They are substantially aimed at minimising the bending of the structural components, and at generating structures that can be characterised as rigid and inflexible, avoiding elasticity. Disastrous failures of conventional structures (for instance under conditions of seismic activity, unusually strong wind forces or unusually heavy snowfall) are revealing the necessity to rethink these paradigms of stiffness and efficiency and try to find a new approach in the conception of structures. Here, textile techniques, especially the way they are deployed in basketry, provide interesting perspectives. They offer high-resolution networks composed of many individual components. A woven system offers the advantage that the failure of singular elements does not trigger the failure of the entire system. Such structures admit large deformation without rupture, a property which is highly unconventional for civil engineering structures. The use of such surface elements can also improve safety considerations with respect to fire, since a prismatic section of a truss of traditional carpentry for instance can be replaced by a multitude of surface elements retaining the overall integrity of the structure even when substantially damaged.

Improving and expanding the uses of timber and timber derived composites for applications in construction and design

For centuries, timber construction and carpentry have been defined by structures made out of simple rectilinear elements, but the field could be transformed by a wide range of new applications that are becoming feasible because of the development of new digital tools. Potentially producible constructions may first emerge as virtual representations, posing a range of new challenges for civil engineering.

The proposed use of planar structural elements and of curved linear elements made out of timber derived products will help introduce timber in structures such as public buildings, where architectural and aesthetic considerations are of strong cultural importance. In the product sector of backfill, insulation, and cladding, high-performance and economically attractive ready-to-build-systems can be developed from the basic principles that are described in this chapter. Other applications within the fields of architecture and design are also possible, although their application in industrial applications has not yet been sufficiently developed.

IBOIS methodology

Deductive methods and inductive methods interact on various levels. For example, the parametric description of a given existing timber fabric can lead to a specific mechanical model with good structural performance first, and only after this, would its potential architectural applications emerge. But a process can also work in the opposite direction: a given form or a weaving technique can be represented with the help of a working model, thus generating a fragment of an entirely new timber fabric (Hudert & Weinand, 2014; Nabaei, 2014). In this scenario, the digital parametric description of the fragment would be developed in the subsequent phase.

The expression 'textile' is not used here in the standard sense of the field of architecture. Instead, the research focuses on the structural description of textiles and their woven aspects in general. Textiles have long attracted the interest of architects, but mainly because of their aesthetic properties. Until now, their structural characteristics and technical particularities have been almost completely neglected. With the recently increasing interest in the use of textile techniques in architectural applications, a need has arisen for in-depth investigation through digital, parametric descriptions and finite element analysis, in order to improve the way textile principles and structures are applied in buildings. Projects like Shigeru Ban's Pompidou Centre in Metz or the railway station in Worb by Swiss architects Smarch are just two examples among many that illustrate the growing relevance of fabrics as references for both structural and aesthetic qualities in architecture.

The research project 'Timber Fabric' improves the understanding of how textiles work, and investigates how to develop existing examples further, by classifying them according to mathematically sound descriptive criteria. It also identifies consequences of using different textiles techniques in structural elements for large-scale buildings. In summary, it attempts to address the question of how to translate these techniques into building structures without betraying the basic principles which underlie their desirable attributes. For instance, in fabrics as well as in basketry, the coherence of the yarn elements is governed by laws of friction. The question arises as to whether textile principles can transform building-scale timber into something that is more than merely a metaphor of weaving. The consequences of such an approach might result in something that is not immediately recognised as a textile structure, yet adapts its logic in the most stringent way. This could be achieved by realising the normally curved geometry of yarns in fabric, in an abstract way, with non-curved planar elements.

Novel interwoven timber elements can be employed in ways that have already been validated in civil engineering terms. This is the case when the technique of interweaving creates double curved geometries, which are structurally advantageous. This area of research draws on the large volume of existing literature related to the study of textiles, their historical background, technical aspects, and the study of textile techniques and structures and will gather together the existing knowledge that is salient to the aims of IBOIS.

The structural analysis of woven wood structures necessitates a stage of preliminary investigations. In order to properly establish analytical models of such structures, a clear understanding of their geometry is required. In general, the intention is initially to build such woven structures out of solid timber panels. During the weaving process, those originally planar panels will be deformed in order to match either curved or preferably 'woven' design templates. The imposed deformations on these panels will lead to initial stresses provoked by bending and torsion moments, which will appear in the panels. Specific questions arise such as: Which radius is required? Which curvature can be accepted? Such questions will be addressed by an empirical approach on ready-to-build structures and their close observation in terms of geometry and material properties. The necessary structural investigations that follow will take their directions from this type of preliminary observation. The following selection of case studies will illustrate how integrative concepts have been realised within the research and teaching at IBOIS.

Case study 1: Experimental vault with overlap

Tʜɪs work opens the way to investigate more detailed questions, for example how overlapping connections can be built at a large scale (Figure 4.4). A deeper underlying research question regarding this weaving structure is: How can this structure be dimensioned, considering that the global model depends directly on the local behaviour and mechanical model of that connection? Ultimately, it is the interaction between the global and the local, which can lead to feasibility questions of such large-scale civil engineering structures and their potential application (Weinand, 2010).

Project: This structure was initially designed by Bastien Thorel at Design Studio Weinand (IBOIS – EPFL, 2008 – 2009), an architectural workshop developing discrete architectural geometry.

(a)

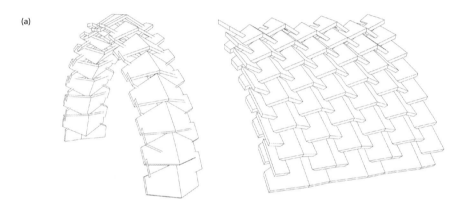

Figure 4.4

a) Axonometric view of the optimized vault and the element's overlapping geometry; b) the realised vault prototype.

Case study 2: Woven arch structure

THE starting point of this case study was examining handmade empirical models and their woven techniques applied to large-scale timber panels (Figure 4.5). Naturally curved patterns are identified and recapitulated out of different materials and at different scales. Local observations of singular points are performed and the structure and geometry is optimised accordingly.

The partial superposition during the interaction of several arches improves the global strength behaviour of the structure. The main structural engineering question concerns the estimation of the surface behaviour. Can the deflection length or buckling criteria for the rising shell be determined? The rigidity of all panels taken together has a higher value than the sum of the rigidities for each panel. This additional stiffness of the global structure needs to be quantified. Ultimately, the initial linear behaviour of arches becomes a surface behaviour of a hybrid shell structure.

Research: Markus Hudert, Timberfabric: Applying Textile Assembly Principles for Wood Construction in Architecture, Thesis n° 5553, EPFL, 2013.

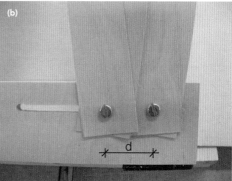

Figure 4.5

a) Experimental models with different woven structures; b) fixations of the woven structures; c) realised timber fabric prototype.

Case study 3: Woven market roof

AGAIN, the starting point was an exploration of weaving techniques. In this instance it led to a first working model with interesting light transmission properties and architectural qualities, which was subsequently applied to light-transmitting roof structures (Figure 4.6).

The failure of one of the 24m long panels (having a section of 3cm by 30cm) will not result in the collapse of the structure as a whole. This research led to the following question: How can the security factor of this specific structure be calculated with the probabilistic method? Such calculations are presently made for major civil engineering structures such as dams, but not for specific buildings. However, for this structure it would be of interest to calculate its specific security factor, taking into account the probabilistic aspects of the multi-layered plywood panel.

Project: Raw like sushi. This project was designed by Sophie Carpentieri, during an architectural workshop, the Design Studio Weinand at IBOIS-EPFL, in 2006–2007.

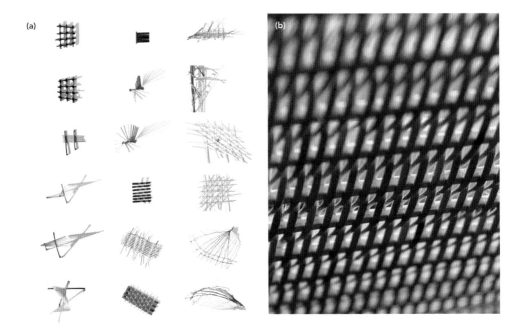

Figure 4.6

a) Experimental digital and physical investigations; b) architectural model of the roof structure and analysis of light transmission.

Case study 4: Curved box beams

THIS research intends to replace a primary and secondary bearing structure by one single structure made out of box beams (Figure 4.7). Those beam sections can be adapted regarding structural requirements, natural light requirements, and acoustic requirements (Humbert, Weinand & Buri, 2012).

Each curved panel will be connected using only wood–wood joints. The parameterisation of the beam's global form and the parameterisation of the wood–wood connections are linked (Robeller, 2015).

Research: Hani Buri, Origami – Folded Plate Structures, Thesis n° 4714, EPFL, 2010.

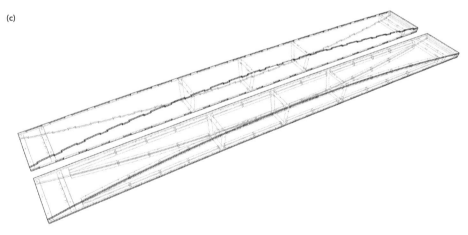

Figure 4.7

a) Experimental investigations; b) prototype of 12m long box beams; c) parametric drawing of the connection details.

Conclusion

THE interdisciplinary research of IBOIS not only brings together architects and engineers, but also relates to social sciences and humanities, as the aesthetic quality of newly developed structures and forms is of significant influence on the social acceptance of their application on a building scale. Investigations on textile techniques and understanding the resulting aesthetic qualities are essential in order to propose structures that are feasible and useful for society. This research, if successful, will offer numerous future opportunities for civil engineering and architectural applications.

References

Hudert, M. & Weinand, Y. (2014). Timberfabric – Textile Assembly Principles and Wood Construction. In G.H. Filz, R. Maleczek, C. Scheiber & C. Gengnagel (eds), *Form – Rule/Rule – Form/2013* (pp. 30–35). Innsbruck: Innsbruck University Press.

Humbert, L., Weinand, Y. & Buri, H.U. (2012). *Curved Origami Beams*. SAH Statusseminar 2012. Ittigen. 24 April 2012.

Nabaei, S.S. (2014). *Mechanical Form-finding of Timber Fabric Structures*. PhD Thesis, École Polytechnique Fédérale de Lausanne, Lausanne.

Robeller, C. (2015). *Integral Mechanical Attachment for Timber Folded Plate Structures*. PhD Thesis, École Polytechnique Fédérale de Lausanne, Lausanne.

Weinand, Y. (2010). *Timber Project – Nouvelles Formes d'Architecture en Bois*. Presses polytechniques et universitaires romandes.

5

Integral joints for timber folded plate structures

Christopher Robeller, Yves Weinand

IBOIS Laboratory for Timber Constructions, EPFL, Switzerland

THE latest developments of research pursued at IBOIS into the *integral attachment* of timber plates opens up new structural typologies for timber, which, as of today, have been limited to steel-reinforced and in-situ cast concrete structures. In their article, authors Christopher Robeller, PhD, and Yves Weinand, director of IBOIS, briefly trace the history of folded plate structures from their origin in the early 1900s, their proliferation and decline, to their current resurgence in the context of timber plate structures. They show how these novel timber structures, enabled by the advent of both new engineered timber panels and numerically controlled fabrication technology, have the potential to combine the efficient form of folded plates with the sustainable credentials of wood. Through built prototypes, they demonstrate how CNC-fabricated dovetail joints inspired by the sophisticated joinery techniques in traditional cabinetmaking can be used not only for the load transfer between the plates, but also for the fast and precise assembly of irregular shaped segmented shells in architecture.

Timber folded plate structures

FOLDED plate structures are so-called surface-active structures, which allow for the construction of self-supporting, column-free segmented shells over large spans with relatively thin plates. Due to their folded shape, they provide a threefold load-bearing action, combining a slab-action, a plate-action and frame-action.

The structural principle originates in constructions with steel-reinforced concrete, which was already a well-developed construction method around 1920. The concept of folded or hipped plates was discovered in the construction of coal bunkers, where steel-reinforced concrete plates were used in a folded configuration (Ehlers, 1930). While early versions of these coal bunkers used additional cross-bracing elements on the inside, these elements were reduced and finally removed entirely in later constructions once the engineers had noticed that the folded shape of the jointed plates performed as a surface-active structure system. This new construction method took particular advantage of the possibility to create quasi-seamless joints with in-situ cast concrete, which allowed for the rigid connections along the edges of the plates that were required to provide the surface-active behaviour of the structure system.

In the following decades, several folded plate structures were built with concrete. However, the construction of these in-situ cast folded plates and other, competing types of concrete shells was labour intensive. Many of the well-known examples were built in Latin-American countries, where the cost of labour was comparably low (Ketchum, 2009). It was also the beginning of prefabrication methods such as precast and pre-stressed concrete, which allowed for a more efficient on-site assembly of building components (Harry, 1963).

The construction of folded plates from discrete components, which allowed for prefabrication but required joints between the individual plates, became popular. Several methods were developed for constructions with concrete and other, newer materials, such as fibre-reinforced composites, which provided a translucent sheet material with a low weight and a high strength. Particularly notable research on folded surface structures built from fibre-reinforced plastics was carried out by the research group of Z.S. Makowski at the University of Surrey in the United Kingdom. Figure 5.1a shows a prototype that was built in 1965, which demonstrates an entirely new topology of a bidirectionally folded cylindrical vault, which allowed for the construction of larger shells from many small, easy-to-handle components.

Further research on these structures was carried out by Pieter Huybers, who illustrated and described the structural principle of what he refers to as antiprismatic shells (Huybers, 1972). Figure 5.1b shows how the alternating, diagonal connection of the members provides cross-bracing, which makes these antiprismatic folded plates an efficient structural system.

Another alternative material, which provides benefits similar to the fibre-reinforced composites, such as the availability in larger sheets and a favourable weight-to-strength ratio, is cross-laminated wood panels, such as plywood. In addition to these advantages, which make the panels an ideal product for prefabricated constructions, the use of wood as a construction material

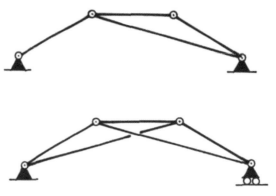

Figure 5.1
Bidirectionally folded antiprismatic cylindrical vaults.

Figure 5.2
Origami-inspired timber folded plate structure, (a) prototype structure, (b) miter-joint with screws.

allows for sustainable constructions. The low energy production and carbon dioxide storage of these wood panels falls in line with the current discourse on sustainability, one of the most important challenges of contemporary building constructions.

A bidirectionally folded surface structure built with cross-laminated wood panels was investigated at the Laboratory for Timber Constructions IBOIS in 2006 (Buri & Weinand, 2006). The experimental cylindrical vault prototype (Figure 5.2) was inspired by the Japanese 'Miura-Ori' origami paper folds and assembled from 124 equally shaped quadrilateral plywood components, which were connected with mitre-joints and crosswise-positioned self-tapping screws.

The load-bearing behaviour of this prototype was investigated, comparing the results of an experimental load test, in which a load was applied to the built prototype until failure, with those of finite-element simulations that assumed rigid joints between the plate components. The analysis demonstrated the generally semi-rigid behaviour of the joints used in this prototype and it was concluded that the overall structural performance of such timber folded plate vaults could be improved through more stiff and rigid connections.

A resurgence of integral timber joints

Tʜᴇ joints of timber constructions have been influenced by technological advances in the history of fabrication methods. For a long time, joints were crafted with hand operated tools such as axes, saws and chisels. Typical joints that were fabricated with these tools, such as mortise-and-tenons, lap-joints or birdsmouth joints, are so-called integral joints, where stresses between the parts are transferred through geometrical features. The form of the parts is used to establish the connection.

During the industrialisation, mass-production technology proliferated quickly and began to replace many of the traditional, integral joinery techniques, which were time-consuming and laborious in their manual production and had become infeasible. The integral techniques were widely replaced by mass-produced mechanical fasteners, such as nails, screws, metal-plate connectors and nail-plates. These connectors did not necessarily provide generally stronger and better joints, but their fabrication could be automated with the newly available technology. A considerable part of the joinery process was moved away from the site into a prefabrication environment. This made the on-site assembly, which is often carried out under difficult environmental conditions, faster and simpler. The assembly with metal fasteners required less experienced and skilled workers on site.

However, with the invention of numerically controlled fabrication technology, another revolutionary technology was introduced. In contrast to the mass-production technology, which was able to produce larger batches of geometrically identical parts, the numerically controlled machines allowed for the efficient production of variation between parts based on corresponding variation in fabrication information.

In the timber construction industry numerically controlled fabrication technology began to proliferate only in the 1970s. Automatic joinery machines, which were capable of fabricating customised integral joints much like the hand-crafted versions before the industrial revolution were developed in the 1980s. With the increasing demand for prefabrication the replacement of manual labour with fabrication technology and the constant improvement of machines, computers, and software, the automatic production of integral joints became a commonly used state-of-the-art technology during the 2000s, which can be considered a resurgence of integral joints for timber frame constructions.

Integral joints for timber plates

For the previously discussed engineered wood panels the situation is slightly different as traditional timber construction did not make use of plate elements. Timber frame constructions used linear elements such as beams and posts, and diagonal beams were used for the structurally necessary cross-bracing. With the invention of cross-laminated structural wood panels the formerly used diagonal beams were replaced by plates, which provided an enclosure and cross-bracing at the same time. However, joints were not required in between the plates but only between the timber beams and the plates.

Direct connections between plate-shaped elements became necessary with the introduction of new building products such as cross-laminated timber (CLT) or laminated veneer lumber (LVL), where complete buildings or building components are assembled entirely from plate-shaped elements. In typical applications, for example the Kerto RIPA wall and roof components (European Organization for Technical Approvals, 2013), a combination of mechanical fasteners and adhesive bonding provides sufficient joints. The orthogonal edgewise connections are assembled in a prefabrication environment.

However, applications like the previously discussed surface-active plate structures present more challenging connections. They require the connection of a large number of joints with non-orthogonal and variable dihedral angles between the plates, and multiple edges meeting in one point. State-of-the-art connectors such as metal plates and screws are not designed for such customised purposes.

Therefore, it was the objective of this research to use the widely available numerically controlled fabrication technology for wood panels such as 5-axis CNC routers for the fabrication of customized integral plate joints. Inspiration for the development of these joints was not taken from traditional carpentry, where no plates were used, but from traditional cabinetmaking, where plate-to-plate connections were very common, and sophisticated joining methods were developed over centuries.

Multiple-tab-and-slot dovetail joints

In carpentry, dovetail joints use only a single dovetail-shaped tab and slot for the connection of two pieces, whereas traditional cabinetmaking joints use multiple tabs and slots for the connection of wooden plates. These joints were traditionally crafted onto wooden boards where they not only provide a mechanically strong connection for corners but also the shape of the joints prevented deformations of the boards, which occur under relative humidity changes.

From a point of view of contemporary timber construction, dovetail-shaped multiple-tab-and-slot joints present an interesting geometry for two main reasons. For one, previous studies have shown that the application of such joints on spruce plywood provides an even higher strength than those on hardwoods such as oak and ash (Sebera & Šimek, 2010). The joints are therefore generally suitable for cross-laminated wood panels. And in contrast to timber boards, where dovetail joints can only be crafted onto the two end-grain edges, perpendicular to the wood fibre, the cross-lamination of plywood allows for the application of the joints on all of the edges of various polygonal shapes.

Due to the shape of the dovetails, which form a prism with their inclined sides, the joints can only be assembled along a single translational direction. This geometry blocks all relative movements between the jointed parts except for this single insertion vector. The joints can therefore transfer various stresses between the parts, such as in-plane and out-of-plane shear forces, and traction or bending moments, all of which occur in bidirectionally folded timber folded plate structures.

Apart from the transfer of stresses through the so-called connector-features, the single insertion direction of the parts plays an important role in the assembly of timber folded plate structures, which often consist of a large number of parts with different dihedral angles, edge lengths, or plate shapes. Such single-degree-of-freedom (1DOF) joints allow for the embedment, or encoding, of the unique and correct alignment and position of the parts into the connection through so-called locator-features. The assembly can be carried out simply, rapidly and with high precision.

Application to timber folded plates

For the application of these joints to a bidirectionally folded timber plate structure, certain challenges and constraints in the fabrication and assembly must be considered. For example, the geometry of the joints had to be adapted for cross-laminated panels and for the cylindrical cutting tools. It required a 5-axis CNC router, as well as a customized algorithm for the generation of the machine code for simultaneous processing, which was implemented with the Application Programming Interface of available CAD software.

The customised fabrication method also included certain constraints. First and foremost a limitation of the maximum tool inclination, from which a minimum and maximum value for the dihedral angles was obtained that could be addressed with these joints. This constrained range of about 40 to 140 degrees, however, still provides a comfortable range for geometrical variations, which also coincides with the structurally ideal angles of a folded surface structure.

The most challenging constraint was presented by the assembly of the joints, which is constrained to only a single direction per edge. This becomes problematic, as soon as the insertion of a plate requires the simultaneous assembly of two or three non-parallel edges, which is the case in every second assembly step in antiprismatic or Miura-Ori based folded surface structures. The assembly direction of traditional European dovetail joints is perpendicular to the edge and lies on one of the two jointed plates (Figure 5.3a). This was sufficient for the applications in traditional cabinetmaking, where the joints were applied to ring-shaped assemblies with parallel edges, such as drawers or cabinets. However, the application of these joints to a plate with three non-parallel edges in the folded plate structure would result in three different assembly directions, which could never be inserted simultaneously.

A solution to this problem was found in traditional Japanese joinery, where so-called Nejiri Arigata joints (Figure 5.3b) demonstrate the diagonal assembly of two plates, with a 1DOF joint geometry. The assembly direction of these joints does not lie on either of the two plates. In contrast to the European joints, which use only a single pin to form a prismatic cross-section profile, the Japanese joints use multiple differently shaped pins. The joints take advantage of their multiple tabs and slots.

In fact, this out-of-plane assembly direction allows not only for the diagonal assembly demonstrated by the Nejiri Arigata joints, but for an arbitrary rotation of the assembly vector, within a range of 180 degrees minus the dihedral angle between the plates. Thus, the range is large for acute and small for obtuse folds. (Figure 4a, θ_1). Furthermore, a rotation to the side (Figure 5.4a, θ_2) is also possible, within a range that is constrained by multiple other parameters.

These two constrained rotations define a three-dimensional, pyramid-shaped rotation

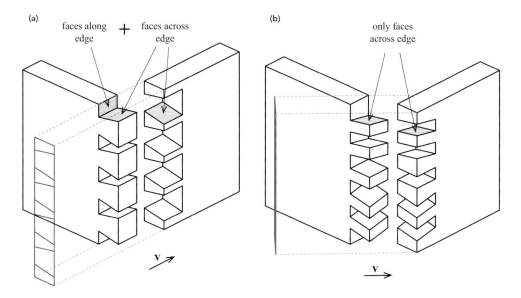

Figure 5.3
Comparison of a European Dovetail and a Japanese Nejiri Arigata joint.

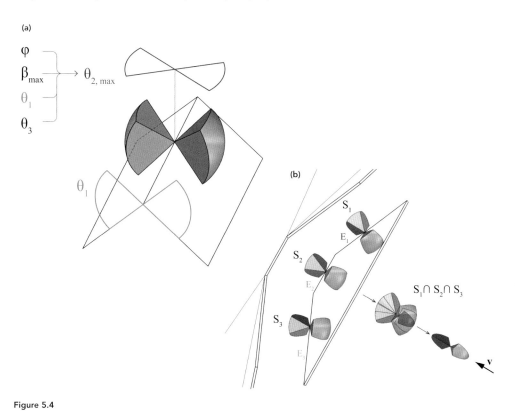

Figure 5.4
3D rotation windows illustrate all possible assembly directions for a joint: a) 3D rotation window;
b) intersection of rotation windows.

Christopher Robeller, Yves Weinand

window, which illustrates all possible assembly directions for this joint. This information is crucial when assembling multiple joints simultaneously. Figure 5.4b shows the rotation windows of three non-parallel edges on the same plate. On the right side, the intersection of these three windows shows all the possible common assembly directions for these three edges, and therefore all possible assembly directions of this part. To verify this new joining method, a bidirectionally arch prototype was built (Figure 5.5). Figure 5.5a demonstrates how a part is inserted.

Due to the different assembly directions, a unique sequence must be planned and followed for the assembly of the parts; however, this could be used as a very beneficial feature where the parts interlock with one another and block their assembly direction. No additional fasteners such as screws or glue were used for this prototype, which was also load-tested and showed a very high stiffness. Under a load equivalent to its self-weight, a deflection of only 1/750 of its span was measured.

While this first prototype was a cylindrical shell with only a single curvature, the algorithmic tools and methods used for the generation and fabrication of the joints allowed for the fabrication of a more advanced prototype with a double-curvature (Figures 5.6 and 5.7) in a second step.

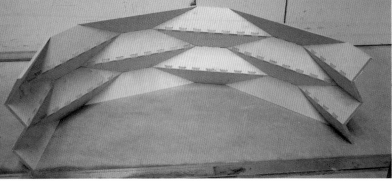

Figure 5.5
Arch prototype, built for the verification of the new assembly method.

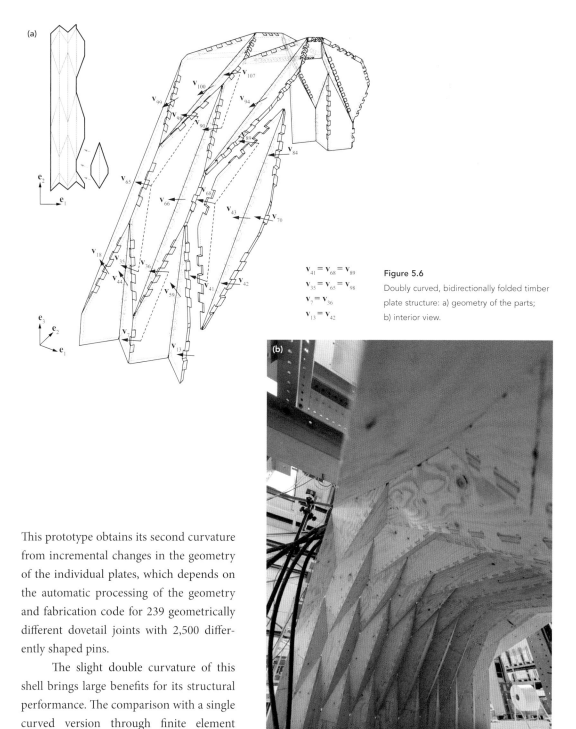

(a)

$\mathbf{e}_2$
$\mathbf{e}_1$

$\mathbf{e}_3$
$\mathbf{e}_2$
$\mathbf{e}_1$

$\mathbf{v}_{41} = \mathbf{v}_{68} = \mathbf{v}_{89}$

$\mathbf{v}_{35} = \mathbf{v}_{65} = \mathbf{v}_{98}$

$\mathbf{v}_7 = \mathbf{v}_{36}$

$\mathbf{v}_{13} = \mathbf{v}_{42}$

Figure 5.6

Doubly curved, bidirectionally folded timber plate structure: a) geometry of the parts; b) interior view.

This prototype obtains its second curvature from incremental changes in the geometry of the individual plates, which depends on the automatic processing of the geometry and fabrication code for 239 geometrically different dovetail joints with 2,500 differently shaped pins.

The slight double curvature of this shell brings large benefits for its structural performance. The comparison with a single curved version through finite element models showed that the deflections under an asymmetrical load such as snow are reduced by 39%.

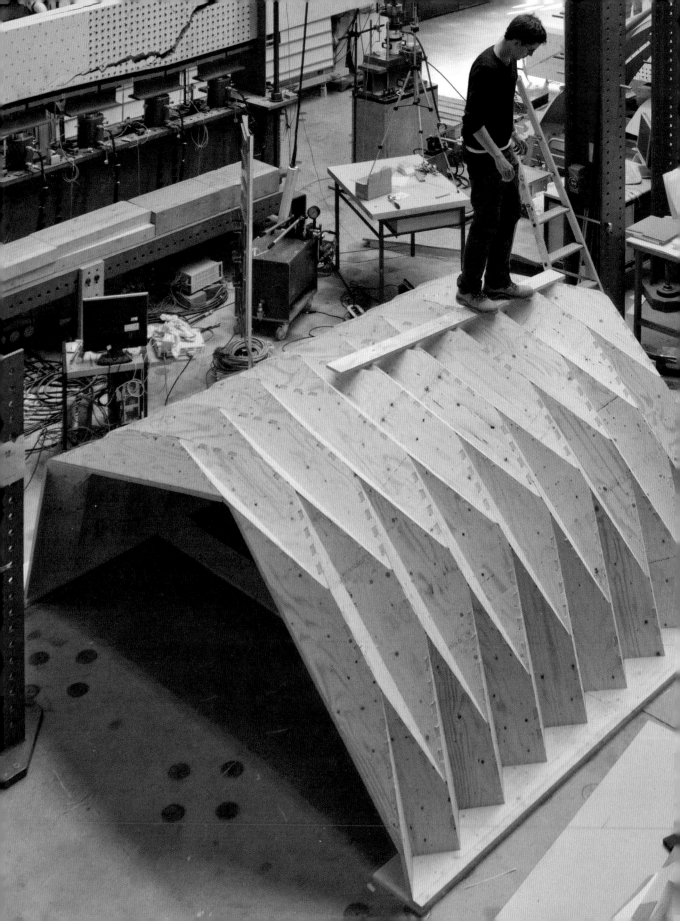

Conclusion

THE research in this chapter presents a step towards the construction of larger, structurally efficient, wide-spanning folded plate structures with aesthetic values, built from a highly sustainable and lightweight material. The manufacturing method takes advantage of both advanced fabrication technology, such as the 5-axis CNC router, which are readily available in modern timber construction companies, and digital geometry processing, which allows for the automatic generation of the geometry of parts and fabrication data.

The development of the joints was inspired by the sophisticated joinery techniques in traditional cabinetmaking, and combines the advantages of traditional joints with those of computer-controlled fabrication technology. A solution for the simultaneous jointing of multiple non-parallel edges was presented through a three-dimensional visualisation of the fabrication and assembly constraints of the 1DOF joint, which proposes a possible strategy for the integration of complex joints into the form-finding process of an architectural design.

References

Buri H. & Weinand Y. (2006). *BSP Visionen – Faltwerkkonstruktionen aus BSP Elementen.* In Grazer Holzbau-Fachtage, Graz.

Ehlers, G. (1930). Ein neues Konstruktionsprinzip. *Bauingenieur*, (1), 125–127.

European Organization for Technical Approvals (2013). *Eta-07/0029 Kerto Ripa Elements – Wood Based Composite Slab Element for Structural Purposes.*

Harry, W.C. (1963). Precast Folded Plates Become Standard Products. *Journal of the American Concrete Institute*, 60(10), 1375–1388.

Huybers, P. (1972). *See-through Structuring: A Method for Large Span Plastics Roofs* (PhD Thesis). Technische Hogeschool Delft, Delft.

Ketchum, M. (2009). What Happened to Shells? 24 October. Retrieved from http://www.ketchum. org/-milo/what.html.

Sebera, V. & Šimek, M. (2010). Finite Element Analysis of Dovetail Joint Made with the Use of CNC Technology. *Acta Universitatis Agriculturae et Silviculturae Mendelianae Brunensis*, 58(5), 321–328.

Figure 5.7 (facing page)
Doubly curved, bidirectionally folded timber plate structure.

6

A hybrid simulation workflow for timber fabric structures

Sina Nabaei,[1] Olivier Baverel,[2] Yves Weinand[3]

[1]BG Consulting Engineers, Switzerland
[2]Navier Research Unit, Ecole des Ponts ParisTech (ENPC), France
[3]IBOIS Laboratory of Timber Constructions, EPFL, Switzerland

Form finding and structural analysis of elastically deformed timber structures, such as the timber fabric structures explored at the Timber Construction Laboratory, IBOIS, challenge established methods of simulation and analysis. Sina Nabaei, PhD, Olivier Baverel, PhD, and Yves Weinand, director of IBOIS, present a novel approach for simulating and analysing such structures that hybridises physics-based form-finding methods borrowed from computer graphics, the structural logic of reciprocal structures, textile inspired interlacing of structural members, and rigorous Finite Element Analysis (FEA). The result is a custom simulation and analysis workflow that takes the non-linearity of the simulation problem into account, while at the same time simplifying the structural simulation and analysis. This opens up possibilities for a whole new family of timber structures, in which the geometry is form-found and behaviour-based.

A hybrid approach

This study brings together two physics-based models, respectively introduced for thin rod and thin plate simulation, and integrates them into a hybrid form-finding pipeline for timber fabric structures (TFS).

While reproducing a braided configuration of panels with flexural resistance, four nonlinear problems have to be solved consecutively: (1) the flexural buckling of an initially flat panel (the solution is known as Euler's Elastica), (2) the rest shape of a clamped panel while either of its ends is twisted, (3) the rest shape of a system of panels under a set of overlap order constraints, and (4) solving for an intersection-free system of deformed panels while respecting the imposed overlap order constraints.

The hybrid approach takes advantage of both kinematic models (rod and plate), and both simulation frameworks (static and pseudo-dynamic) depending on the physical problem to simulate. Buckling, twisting and interlacing are handled using a constrained elastic energy minimisation framework, whereas intersection resolving uses a pseudo-dynamically integrated thin plate framework. It is finally demonstrated that once fine-tuned, these physics-based models can considerably simplify the Finite Element Method (FEM) simulation of TFS by providing a prediction of the expected curved geometry.

Overview

TIMBER fabric structures originate from an architectural research project at IBOIS-EPFL, looking into the application of textile principles at building scale in the particular context of timber construction (Hudert, 2012; Weinand & Hudert, 2010). The main components of this interdisciplinary research have been flexible timber panels and their assembly logic, the former being inspired by its textile microstructure. The idea suggests an immediate generalisation: What would be the relaxed geometry of a set of flexible panels under a given set of interlace boundary conditions of, for example, a three-strand braid?

A proper formulation and a computational framework have to be developed consequently. This computational revisit becomes inevitable once a general interlaced configuration is to be investigated with an arbitrarily chosen design pattern, with an unlimited number of overlapping panels and various cross sections and elastic properties (Figure 6.1).

Some proper interpretations of interlacing with structural implications appear in reciprocal frame structures (Baverel, 2000). However, there are two main differences between a so-called 'Nexorade' and a TFS. First of all, connected elements of a reciprocal system satisfy the imposed pattern of reciprocity with small deformations and so undergo only a few number of overlaps. The reciprocity in this case is more about the intelligent positioning of components, rather than their deformation. The second difference lies in the continuity. There is a discrete conception inherent in a reciprocal system, making it an assembly of overlapped, but actually discontinuous elements, whereas in the case of the TFS, the use of long flexible elements is promoted and interlacing becomes more fluid. Although different in the self-formation process, node complexity of reciprocal frames inspires TFS concepts. Classical interlaces such as the braided and woven configurations have an alternating set of ordered nodes; following a single component, it passes consecutively on top and under another component at design-specified overlap nodes. The exact notion appears for the reciprocal frames and can inspire new TFS concepts by transforming a reciprocal node into a TFS (Figure 6.2).

Figure 6.1 (facing page, top)
The timber fabric.

Figure 6.2 (facing page, bottom)
Learning from reciprocal frames.

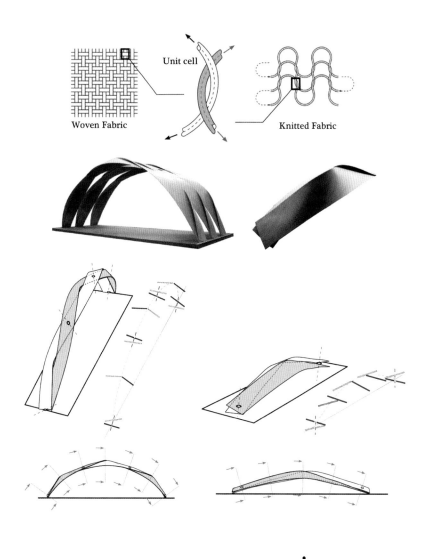

Woven Fabric

Unit cell

Knitted Fabric

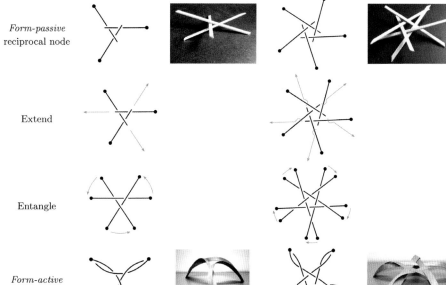

Form-passive reciprocal node

Extend

Entangle

Form-active structure

Physics-based hybrid simulation pipeline

THE complexity of the interlaced structure's form-finding can be reduced by breaking it into pertinent sub-problems. These generic sub-problems are based on the flexible body model used to represent panels and the physical phenomenon to simulate. The flexural/torsional buckling is the key curving agent for the TFS. Supposing a static framework, the buckling of a flat panel into an Elastica can be readily formulated, similar to developments presented in Nabaei, Bavarel & Weinand (2014). A constrained elastic energy minimisation framework seems suitable to handle the TFS buckling problem. The main constraints to deal with are the twisted end edges, panels which have to pass underneath or above each other at a particular position (interlacing), and the imposed total length and span. All of these boundary conditions can be formulated as equality constraints acting on the rod's degrees of freedom.

At this point, if the minimum elastic energy configuration coming out of the optimisation does not contain any intersecting panels, all of the aforementioned constraints can be solved using the rod model. Intersection detection is advantageous because of its plate kinematics in a dynamic simulation, where the information about the vertex trajectory is available. This motivates a hybrid approach, taking advantage of both rod and plate models. A discrete plate dynamic engine presented in Nabaei, Bavarel & Weinand (2015) is able to handle a deformable panel as a discrete mesh. In the case of multiple interacting panels, the integration procedure remains similar to that of single interaction, except for the addition of multiple vertex forces. A simple uniform triangle mesh generator ensures the transformation from the rod solver to the plate solver by averaging the edge material frames to get the cross-section orientation at each rod vertex.

Case studies

TWO case studies are discussed here in order to support the application of the presented form-finding procedure: a trefoil tripod arch and a pentafoil roof. In both examples, panels are supposed to be made from timber with homogeneous elastic properties.

An interlaced trefoil

THE concept structure illustrated in Figure 6.3 is an example of interlacing which requires an intersection handling step. The trefoil arch structure is supposed to be made with timber panels 0.24m × 0.015m. All panels are 14m long and span over 8.5m. Respective twist of (-15°, -30°) is applied on start and end vertices of each panel. At its intersection-free relaxed state, the arch is 4.8m high at its middle vertex. Similar to a knot, the order of overlap can be marked with a positive or negative linking number. Based on the same interlaced diagram of trefoil arch structure, two dual structures would exist, interpreting this variation of linking number (Figure 6.4).

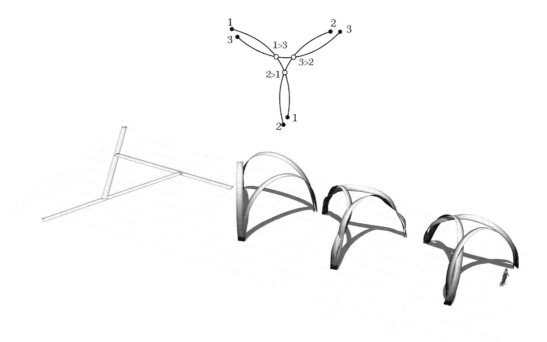

Figure 6.3

A trefoil interlaced arch structure with colliding panels: (left to right)initial flat configuration, the solution to the Elastica problem, interlaced configuration (contains intersection), intersections handled.

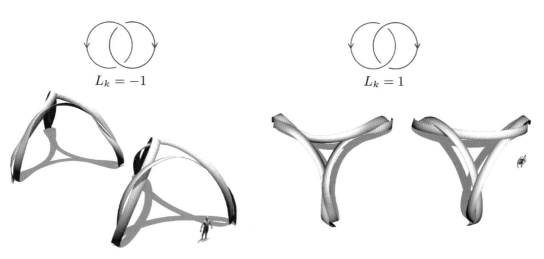

Figure 6.4

Trefoil duals with respect to crossing's linking sign: (top) positive and negative crossing; (bottom) trefoil duals with inversed crossing sign.

An interlaced pentafoil

Tʜᴇ concept structure illustrated in Figure 6.5 is a complex TFS with multiple overlap nodes and colliding components. The pentafoil roof structure is made from timber panels 0.65m × 0.03m, all 14m long spanning over 11.8m with support points equally spaced on a circle of 6.3m radius and its 0.2m offset. Respective twist of (34°, 34°) is applied on start and end vertices of each panel. As a result of interlacing, the arch lifts up to clear 1.98m vertically with respect to the support point at its intersection-free relaxed state.

FEM simulation of TFS revisited

Hʏʙʀɪᴅ physics-based form-finding can considerably simplify the FEM simulation procedure for a TFS by providing a predicted relaxed assembly. By generating form-found geometry using the physics-based simulation pipeline, the exact assembly sequence of flat panels is no longer needed for the FEA. Instead of a chain of numerous simulations for assembly steps, the process can be simplified into a two-step procedure of assembly and relaxation. The vertices at overlaps have already been determined by the user while interlacing, and with the form-found geometry, a close prediction of the relaxed position of these vertices, as well as mesh normal vectors is now available. Therefore, instead of simulating the braiding procedure step by step, the output geometry of the form-finding pipeline is used as a reference for a preliminary assembly step where flat panels are pulled with axial wires from these coupled vertices into the predicted form-found coordinates. Once overlapped vertices are positioned at their form-found coordinates, a second step of Finite Element Analysis is launched, coupling overlapping vertices in order to maintain their relative local setting while the connected system is relaxed during a pseudo-dynamic step. The core advantage of this procedure is that there is no need for contact handling in the preliminary assembly simulation step: panels are allowed to traverse each other and reach the form-found coordinates. The contact handling is only activated during the final relaxation step.

Figure 6.5

A pentafoil interlaced roof with multiple colliding panels: (left to right) initial flat configuration, the solution to the Elastica problem, interlaced configuration (contains intersection), intersections handled.

This approach is applied to the complex case of a pentafoil roof structure. The assembly and relaxation simulation settings are sketched in Figure 6.6 with axial connector wires highlighting the mesh vertices used as handles to deform flat panels. The flat initial configuration is incrementally dragged into the reference positions. The difference between the deformed configuration corresponding to the end of the assembly step (red) and the result of the relaxation step (black) is also shown in Figure 6.7. The structure self-reconfigures and bends slightly inward due to interaction of the coupled and contacting panels. The variation of the kinetic energy, internal energy and the viscous dissipated energy are also reported for both steps combined ($0 \leq t \leq 10$ for assembly and $10 \leq t \leq 12$ for relaxation), ensuring that the assembly has reached the steady state at the end of the relaxation step. The result of the physics-based simulation turns out to be a close prediction of the relaxed assembly, confirming the pertinence of the procedure.

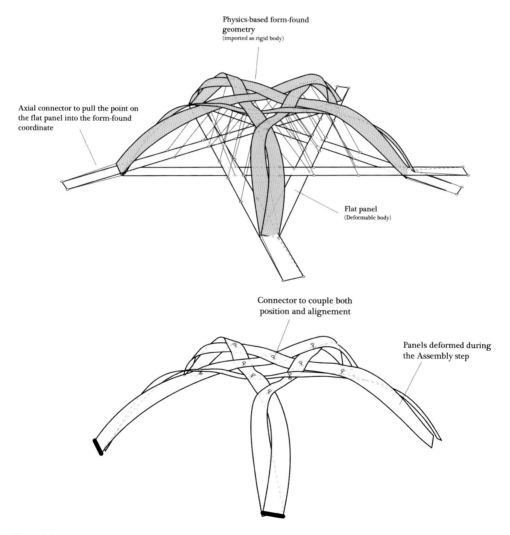

Physics-based form-found geometry
(imported as rigid body)

Axial connector to pull the point on the flat panel into the form-found coordinate

Flat panel
(Deformable body)

Connector to couple both position and alignement

Panels deformed during the Assembly step

Figure 6.6
FEM simulation step setting for pentafoil roof structural analysis.

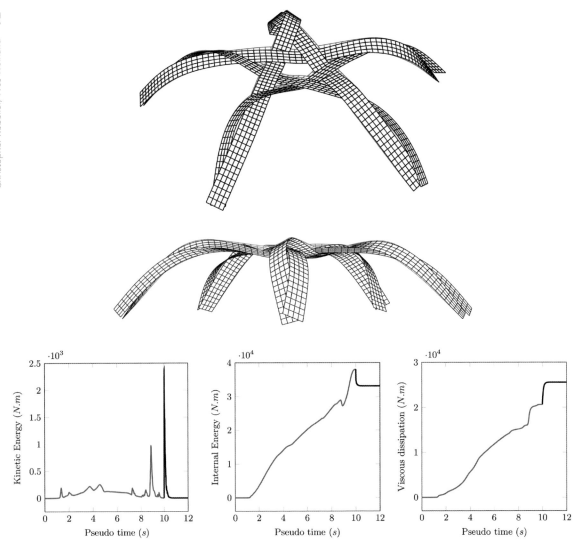

Figure 6.7

Deformed mesh comparison between FEM simulation steps comparing beginning (red) and the end of relaxation (black).

Conclusion

THIN panels can be simulated as both rods with rectangular cross-sections and thin plates. A form-finding framework may either be a nonlinear static simulation or a pseudo-dynamic simulation. The hybrid solution presented here leverages the advantages of both models and frameworks in relation to the simulated physical phenomenon.

Buckling a flat panel by displacing its end vertices, twisting this buckled configuration and connecting several of these panels using kinematic constraints for proximity and alignment can all be comfortably realised using a rod model. Since only the final deformed configuration matters, a static nonlinear framework can be used. Additionally, an intersection resolving method that is specific to the TFS is used. It is easier to deal with 2D geometry (a mesh) than with 1D geometry (a curve). The transition from rod solver to plate solver is realised by generating a regular mesh from the rod's deformed and initial configurations, using the fact that panels are deformed from a flat initial configuration.

A number of nonlinear solvers have been configured as building blocks that form a toolbox. These blocks can be used to implement the proposed pipeline for creating TFS. However, the toolbox is designed in such a way that other potential problems that are ruled by similar logics can be explored as well.

Aside from form exploration purposes, the prediction of the relaxed geometry of a TFS assembly assists the FEA by providing a reference deformation of the panel geometry. Instead of calculating deformation according to an assembly operation such as braiding, the FEA is simplified by pulling the vertices of flat panels to coordinates that are the result of the first stage physics-based prediction. Overlapping vertices are then coupled before letting the system reach a state of equilibrium. Both the assembly and the relaxation stages are pseudo-dynamic simulations using FE shell elements.

Acknowledgments

THIS work was sponsored by the Swiss National Science Foundation (SNSF) under grant No. 200021 137884/1. This support is gratefully acknowledged. The authors would also like to thank Basile Audoly and Eitan Grinspun for their constructive remarks on problem formulation and implementation.

References

Hudert, M. (2012). *Structural Timber Fabric: Applying Textile Principles in Building Scale.* PhD Thesis, École Polytechnique Fédérale de Lausanne, Lausanne.

Nabaei, S.S., Baverel, O. & Weinand, Y. (2014). Form-Finding of Interlaced Space Structures. In E. Onate, J. Oliver & A. Huerta (eds), *11th World Congress on Computational Mechanics.* 20–25 July, Barcelona, Spain.

Nabaei, S.S., Baverel, O. & Weinand, Y. (2015). Form Finding of Twisted Interlaced Structures: A Hybrid Approach. In P. Block, J. Knippers, N.J. Mitra & W. Wang (eds), *Advances in Architectural Geometry 2014* (pp. 127–143). London: Springer.

Weinand, Y. & Hudert, M. (2010). Timberfabric: Applying Textile Principles on a Building Scale. *Architectural Design,* 80(4), 102–107.

PART THREE

Institute for Computational Design, University of Stuttgart, Germany

7

Integrative design computation for advancing wood architecture

Achim Menges

Institute for Computational Design, University of Stuttgart, Germany

Wood differs from most other building materials. Instead of being industrially produced according to the specific requirements of the building industry, wood is a natural tissue that grows in response to the biological requirements of trees. From a material science point of view, wood can be described as a natural cellulose-reinforced composite material with a highly differentiated internal structure. As a consequence most properties of wood are directly rooted in the microscopic make-up of the material and its natural origin. The architects' stance towards the biological basis of wood has changed considerably across different eras of technological and cultural development, oscillating between an unconditional acceptance as one of the most common building materials in pre-industrial times, to general neglect and a renewed appreciation today. Achim Menges, director of the Institute for Computational Design at the University of Stuttgart, introduces three research areas that aim at advancing wood architecture through the integration and synthesis of fundamental wood characteristics in computational design, simulation and fabrication processes.

Wood characteristics – computational integration

Until the dawn of industrialisation, the availability and natural renewability of wood, in combination with its excellent workability and the related long-standing tradition of craftsmanship, led to it being one of the most common and frequently used materials. Almost any manmade artefact ranging from basic articles of daily use to architecture was made from wood. However, in the relatively short period of just a few decades the pre-eminence of wood was superseded by more modern materials that were thought to be better suited to the challenges of new modes of production and the related reorganisation of labour. Guild-based crafts rooted in medieval times struggled to adapt to the rising of mechanisation. At the same time wood faced increasing competition from cast iron, steel, glass and eventually reinforced concrete. Because these materials were technologically produced and specifically developed for the building sector, they showed a much higher level of consistency and homogeneity. In a technological context of increasing industrialisation and the related need for standardisation and regulation these characteristics were regarded superior to the inherent heterogeneity and biological variability of wood.

Today, the way wood is seen as a construction material undergoes yet another significant change. One obvious reason is that the building sector faces the very serious need to substantially reduce its environmental impact, as it contributes a major part to global energy consumption, CO_2 emission and waste production. Given these circumstances, wood is experiencing renewed interest as a construction material with unrivalled ecological virtues. It holds a very low level of embodied energy and it also has a positive carbon footprint (Kolb, 2008), even if today's heavily industrial wood processing is taken into account (Scheer, Feil & Zerwer, 2006). In addition, it constitutes a natural, recyclable and fully renewable resource, at least if grown in sustainable silviculture. Moreover, due to its cellular microstructure with a large percentage of cavities, wood shows by far the best load-bearing capacity of all heat-insulating materials. All in all, it is increasingly recognised that wood is one of the very few truly environmentally sound and highly energy efficient building materials we currently have at our disposal.

Another critical reason for the renewed interest in wood stems from the further advancement of technology. Whereas the first wave of industrialisation entailed a shift away from wood architecture, recent technological progress allows reconnecting the material's inherent capacities with the characteristics of contemporary design and construction processes. In this development computation plays a key role as a decisive enabling technology, because it equips both the designer and the maker with integrative modalities to revisit wood's intricate structure and related complex properties. The Institute for Computational Design (ICD) at the University of Stuttgart has conducted a series of research projects that investigate how recent advances in design computation, simulation and fabrication offer the possibility to revisit the specific nature of the material, which have proven to be quite a challenge in the recent past, as advantageous – and at times even surprising – behavioural capacities and related rich design opportunities. In the following paragraphs the potential of such a computational perspective on advancing wood architecture will be introduced alongside examples of three important characteristics of wood: its machinability, its elasticity and its hygroscopicity.

Machinabilty – fabrication integration

From the beginning of craft the ease of wood working relative to the remarkable characteristics of the resulting artefacts, especially when compared to other naturally available materials, has been recognised and exploited across many different cultures. The combination of workability and machinability, together with excellent mechanical properties such as stiffness and strength as well as the striking haptic and visual qualities of the material, has found its expression in countless

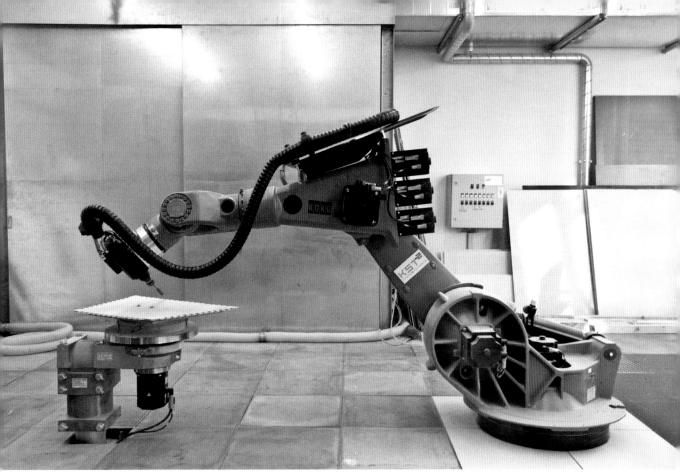

Figure 7.1
Robotic fabrication set-up for the ICD/ITKE Research Pavilion 2011.

traditional wood products and finely detailed timber structures, and the related evolution of a multitude of wood working techniques. Today, computer aided manufacturing (CAM) and robotic fabrication enable us to revisit traditional craft approaches from a computational perspective. One example of transferring long-established techniques into the contemporary realm of computational design and construction are robotically fabricated finger joints, which have been the subject of several years of research at the ICD (Figure 7.1). While still maintaining the traditional finger joints' key advantage of embedding the connection in the building element itself, and thus establishing a mono-material system without the need for additional mechanical fasteners, the robotic fabrication process allows for the jointing of elements of varying thicknesses at a range of different angles (Figure 7.2).

The ICD/ITKE Research Pavilion 2011 investigated the possibility of using plates with robotically fabricated finger joints for constructing architectural-scale plate structures (La Magna et al., 2013). This poses the considerable challenge that, on the one hand, the finger joints are very good in withstanding shear forces along the edge of the plates, but, on the other hand, they are also fairly weak in resisting bending moments or tension forces. Thus the research team of

Figure 7.2

Close-up view of the ICD/ITKE Research Pavilion 2011 revealing the intricate finger joint connections.

architects, engineers and biologists studied natural plate systems that have mastered exactly this challenge. For example, the shell of the Sand Dollar consists of discreet, polygonal plates connected by stereom projections, which are the natural equivalent of man-made finger joints. A set of performative morphological principles were identified and captured in algorithmic design rules. The developed computational process enables the designer to explore the machinic morphospace (Menges, 2013) – that is the design space of robotically producible plate forms – through the filter of the biomimetic rules, which in concert with spatial and contextual criteria leads to a highly specific plate shell. The resulting lightweight, modular wood shell demonstrates both the structural capacity and the architectural potential of a system that entirely consist of 6.5mm thin plywood plates connected by more than 100,000 different, robotically fabricated finger joints (Figure 7.3). The possibility of synthesising resource effectiveness and spatial expression through a higher level of fabrication integration in the computational design of wood architecture was further investigated in *Landesgartenschau Exhibition Hall* project (see Chapter 8), which also allowed the transfer from a research demonstrator to a permanent and fully enclosed building (Figure 7.4).

Figure 7.3 (facing page, top)

The ICD/ITKE Research Pavilion was constructed from 850 different finger-jointed plates.

Figure 7.4 (facing page, bottom)

a) Exterior view of the Landesgartenschau Exhibition Hall. The shell is covered by polygonal cladding. At night the interior is visible through the glass façade. b) The load-carrying plate structure of the pavilion is illuminated by the lighting concept.

(a)   (b)

Elasticity – behaviour integration

COMPUTATION also offers the possibility of integrating material behaviour as an active driver in the design process. Wood's behavioural characteristics stem from its micro- and ultrastructural anatomy. On this level, it is revealed that in the various layers of the wood cells, the cellulosic microfibrils function like 'fibres' that reinforce a 'matrix' of lignin and hemicellulose (Dinwoodie, 2000). Thus wood is often referred to as a natural composite material, and as such it shares a number of characteristics with synthetic composites, such as glass fibre-reinforced plastics (GRP). This is also evident in the fact that many products previously made from wood are now produced in GRP. The pole for pole vaulting is a striking example, and it also highlights the materials' particular stress–strain relation showing a high level of both elasticity and structural capacity.

These material characteristics are especially well suited for construction techniques that employ the elastic behaviour of wood to physically compute form (Figure 7.5). However, despite the fact that the elasticity allows for achieving relatively complex curvature from initially simple planar elements and that it can contribute to significantly increasing structural capacity, it is hardly ever used in architecture. Rare exceptions are the timber grid shells developed by Frei Otto in the 1970s at his institute in Stuttgart, such as the Multihalle in Mannheim built in 1975. Here, the structure was initially assembled as an entirely flat and regular timber lattice, but once it was jacked up at a few strategic points, it found its structurally stable, double curved form based on the elastic behaviour of the wood elements.

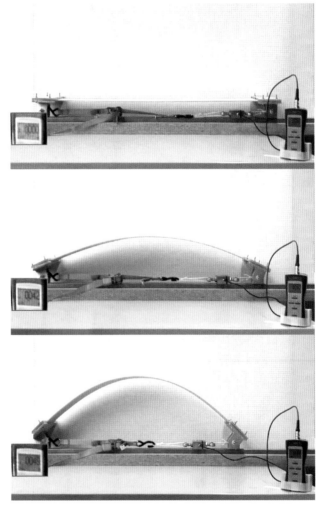

Figure 7.5

The relation between the self-computed bending geometry and applied forces was analysed during the development of the ICD/ITKE Research Pavilion 2010.

Figure 7.6
On-site assembly of the ICD/ITKE Research Pavilion 2010.

The ICD/ITKE Research Pavilion 2010 set out to further develop this lineage of bending-active structures within the context of today's computational design, simulation and fabrication technologies (Fleischmann et al., 2012). The pavilion's structure consists of initially planar, thin plywood strips that are designed to be connected at unequal length intervals, resulting in elastically bent and tensioned regions that alternate along their length (Figure 7.6). The residual stress that is locally stored in each bent region of the strip, and maintained by the corresponding tensioned region of the neighbouring strip, significantly enhances the structural stiffness of this self-equilibrating system. One critical detail here is the lateral connection points between the elements, as the undulation of the strips results in considerably reduced structural depth. However, the computational design process not only allowed for the integration of the elastic material behaviour, it also enabled the algorithmically driven, irregular placement of the joints, so that introducing local irregularity finally leads to global stability (Figure 7.7). During the assembly process, the elastic behaviour of the wooden strips physically computes the pavilion's form, with the final equilibrium state unfolding both a unique architectural space and a highly effective timber structure. In this way, the project demonstrates how focusing the computational design process on material behaviour rather than geometric shape allows for achieving structural capacity and material

Figure 7.7
The undulating connections between the individual strips lead to the pavilion's global stability.

resourcefulness while at the same time expanding the design space towards formerly unexplored architectural possibilities. Here, the material no longer remains a passive receptor of predefined form but rather becomes a truly active generator of design.

Besides the exploration of the elastic bending of linear, strip-shaped elements as in the ICD/ITKE Research Pavilion 2010, the ICD has also investigated conical, plate-shaped elements. This research has resulted in the design and construction of the modular skin of the HygroSkin – Meteorosensitive Pavilion for the FRAC Centre in Orleans (see Chapter 9). In addition, several studies have been conducted to test strategies for modifying the elastic behaviour of wood. Both mechanical manipulations, such as robotic kerfing, or bio-chemical modifications, as for example steaming or local lignin removal, extend the spectrum of design possibilities significantly and allow for the specific differentiation of the elastic material behaviour.

Hygroscopicity – performance integration

I N addition to employing passive material behaviour, such as the elastic formation introduced in the previous paragraphs, computational design and fabrication also allows for the integration of wood's innate performative capacity of self-forming and responsive movements. One mechanism that enables such motion without motors is hygroscopic actuation, which is quite literally engrained in wood's material make-up. Hygroscopicity refers to a material's ability to maintain its moisture content in equilibrium with the surrounding's humidity level (Skaar, 1988). This adsorption and desorption of water molecules results in a differential change of dimensions due to wood's specific anatomy. More often than not, this anisotropic dimensional instability of wood has been understood as a deficiency of the material by craftsmen, engineers and architects alike. In fact, the vast majority of energy consumed during wood processing is invested in suppressing this innate material performance by drying the wood to low moisture content. In stark contrast to this, biology has evolved ingenious ways of utilising hygroscopic behaviour. Conifer cones, as for example pine or spruce cones, are growing in an initially moist, closed state, but when the moisture content reduces they open entirely by themselves. They manage to translate an anisotropic dimensional change of the tissue into a shape change of the scales (Dawson, Vincent & Rocca, 1997), which is a fully reversible movement and solely driven by fluctuations in ambient relative humidity.

The ICD has conducted several years of research studying how wood's inherent moisture-responsiveness can be employed for the design of weather-reactive architectural envelopes (Menges & Reichert, 2012). Based on the biomimetic principle of utilising anisotropic dimensional change to drive movement, veneer-composite elements were developed that adapt their shape to variations in relative humidity without the need for any additional electronic or mechanical equipment. In the computational design and fabrication process this responsive behaviour can be programmed to various response ranges and actions. For example, the exact same system with the same layer-structure and material constituents can be programmed to either open or close during a reduction in moisture content. The related body of research and development work (Reichert, Menges and Correa, 2015) was fully synthesised for the first time in an installation for the permanent collection of the Centre Pompidou in Paris. Built from computationally defined and fabricated veneer-composite elements, the HygroScope – Meteorosensitive Morphology is situated in a large display case (Figure 7.8). Within the glass case the climate corresponds to the relative humidity changes in Paris, to which the system continuously responds, providing a visual experience of the subtle humidity fluctuations that form part of our everyday lives but usually escape our spatial perception. A small increase in relative humidity is sufficient to trigger the system to open, as the simple veneer composite elements embody the capacity to sense, actuate and respond, with no need for any additional mechanical or electronic equipment, or even the supply of operational energy. A subsequent commission to build the HygroSkin – Meteorosensitive Pavilion for the FRAC Centre in Orleans allowed testing a first architectural application. Here, the weather-responsive systems close with an increase in relative humidity (Figure 7.9). On a dry sunny day, the apertures are fully open, but once the weather changes and rain approaches, they shut entirely by themselves, leading to a unique convergence of spatial and environmental experience (Figure 7.10).

Currently the ICD pursues two lines of further research for developing design strategies of deploying hygroscopic actuation in architecture. One field of investigation focuses on further disassembling wood into its basic material constituents – lignin and cellulose – and then reassembling them through 3D-printing processes. This additive manufacturing approach opens up the possibility of achieving more complex movements by designing the micro-structure of the material

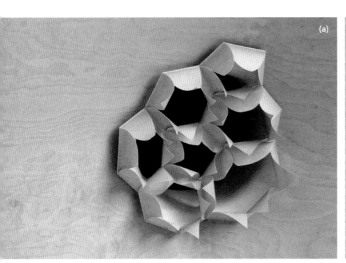 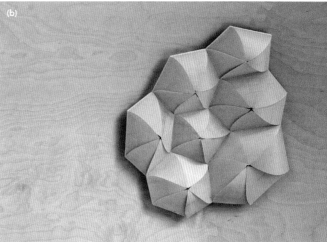

Figure 7.9

The HygroSkin apertures open with decreasing relative humidity (a) and close with increasing relative humidity (b).

Figure 7.10

The HygroSkin – Meteorosensitive Pavilion on the university campus in the morning with high relative humidity.

itself (Figure 7.11). The second area of research studies the use of much thicker wooden bi-layer systems. Here the main emphasis is on developing humidity-driven self-forming processes of large-scale building parts that can be strategically programmed to transform from a flat-packed moist state to more complex element geometry.

Outlook

THE three research areas presented in this paper allowed gaining a deeper insight into how the related three key characteristics of wood can be explored and deployed through computational design, simulation and fabrication. The next step will be to synthesise the as of yet discreet investigations of machinability, elasticity and hygroscopicity into one approach of advancing wood systems and architecture. This will also entail a more comprehensive integration of the biological variability of wood, which no longer needs to be averaged out or glossed over, but can become an integral part of cyber-physical design and production systems that span from scanning the individual material make-up of each piece to its anatomically specific use. Rethinking wood through a computational perspective has only just begun.

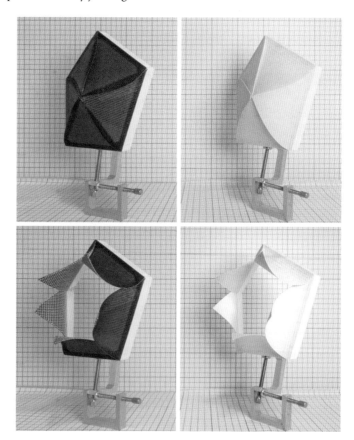

Figure 7.11
Comparison of the hygroscopic behaviour between a 3D-printed component (left) and the regular veneer aperture (right) shows the potential of lignin-based additive manufacturing processes.

Acknowledgments

THE author gratefully acknowledges the work of all researchers and students at the Institute for Computational Design at the University of Stuttgart and the participants in the Performative Wood studios at Harvard Graduate School of Design, who were involved in the projects introduced here. In particular, the author thanks Professor Jan Knippers and all researchers of the Institute of Building Structures and Structural Design who participated in the research pavilion projects in 2010 and 2011, as well as the various collaborating research partners. Finally, the author would like to express his sincere gratitude to the various funding bodies and sponsors who made this work possible and to the University of Stuttgart for providing a stimulating context in which this research can thrive.

References

Dawson, C., Vincent, J.F.V. & Rocca, A.-M. (1997). How Pine Cones Open. *Nature*, 390(6661), 668.

Dinwoodie, J.M. (2000). *Timber, its Nature and Behaviour* (2nd edn). London, New York, England: CRC Press.

Fleischmann, M., Knippers, J., Lienhard, J., Menges, A. & Schleicher, S. (2012). Material Behaviour: Embedding Physical Properties in Computational Design Processes. *Architectural Design*, 82(2), 44–51.

Kolb, J. (2008). *Systems in Timber Engineering: Loadbearing Structures and Component Layers*. Basel: Birkhäuser Basel.

La Magna, R., Gabler, M., Reichert, S., Schwinn, T., Waimer, F., Menges, A. & Knippers, J. (2013). From Nature to Fabrication: Biomimetic Design Principles for the Production of Complex Spatial Structures. *International Journal of Spatial Structures*, 28(01), 27–40.

Menges, A. (2013). Morphospaces of Robotic Fabrication: From Theoretical Morphology to Design Computation and Digital Fabrication in Architecture. In S. Brell-Çokcan & J. Braumann (eds), *Rob/Arch 2012: Robotic Fabrication in Architecture, Art and Design* (pp. 28–47). Vienna: Springer Verlag.

Menges, A. & Reichert, S. (2012). Material Capacity: Embedded Responsiveness. *Architectural Design*, 82(2), 52–59.

Reichert, S., Menges, A. & Correa, D. (2015). Meteorosensitive Architecture: Biomimetic Building Skins Based on Materially Embedded and Hygroscopically Enabled Responsiveness. *CAD Journal*, 60, 50–69.

Scheer, D., Feil, A. & Zerwer, C. (2006). Nachhaltigkeit im Bereich Bauen und Wohnen: ökologische Bewertung der Bauholz-Kette, Institut für ökologische Wirtschaftsforschung. *Arbeitsbericht 8 für die ZUFO Zukunftsmärkte der Forst-Holz-Kette*. Heidelberg.

Skaar, C. (1988). *Springer Series in Wood Science. Wood–Water Relations*. Berlin, Heidelberg: Springer Berlin Heidelberg.

8

Landesgartenschau Exhibition Hall

Tobias Schwinn

Institute for Computational Design, University of Stuttgart, Germany

THE synthesis of material characteristics, computational design and robotic fabrication provides the opportunity for the realisation of timber structures that lie outside the scope of established design conventions and fabrication protocols. In his contribution, Tobias Schwinn, research associate and doctoral candidate at the Institute of Computational Design at the University of Stuttgart, introduces the Landesgartenschau Exhibition Hall, a full-scale building prototype that not only showcases a prototype for an extremely lightweight timber plate system but also a novel method for its computational design and fabrication. The project, which is the outcome of a collaborative research and development project, is characterised by a multidisciplinary approach that concurrently integrates knowledge from different domains such as architectural design, structural engineering, robotic fabrication and geodesy. The integration of these domains, however, transcends the scope of established knowledge-based design approaches and, consequently, a novel behaviour-based and inherently integrative design approach is proposed.

Building prototype

THE Landesgartenschau Exhibition Hall is a permanent, and thus fully enclosed, insulated and waterproof building prototype whose primary structure has been robotically fabricated from regionally sourced beech plywood (Figure 8.1). Following an integrative design approach that involved all stakeholders from the very start of the project, an extraordinarily lightweight timber plate structure was achieved with a structural shell thickness of only 50mm. The project is the outcome of the EU-funded collaborative research project 'Robotics in Timber Construction' and is specifically aimed at a knowledge transfer from research into practice.[1]

Site and brief

THE building was realised within the context of the Landesgartenschau, a horticultural and landscaping expo, in 2014, in Schwäbisch Gmünd, Germany. Completed in spring of the same year, the project's brief was to provide exhibition space that, at a later stage, could be easily converted into an event space including associated facilities. It is located within the park-like setting of the expo site on a plateau above Schwäbisch Gmünd, where it sits next to a dense deciduous forest that connects the park and the city. The forest is home to many of the same native species of beech trees that the exhibition hall itself is made from.

Building and geometry

THE building's architectural character largely stems from the adaptively changing pattern of the polygonal plate outlines, which are the result of a newly developed generation scheme for segmented shell structures (Figure 8.2). The plate outlines thereby reflect the changing Gaussian curvature of the shell surface, which, in turn, retraces the volumes associated with its primary

Figure 8.2

Exterior view of the Landesgartenschau Exhibition Hall showing the adaptively changing plate pattern.

functional zones: the reception area, which the visitor enters through the slightly lower, south-facing facade; and the 6m tall main exhibition area where one arrives after passing through a spatial contraction of the building volume. Through a large glass facade, the main space opens up the view across the surrounding landscape. The result is a continuous shell surface of about 245m² spanning 17 x 11m with two dome-shaped, synclastic surface regions that are separated by a transitional saddle-shaped, anticlastic surface region. Together, both zones provide about 125 m² of usable floor area.

Material and locality

O NE of the most relevant characteristics of timber in the context of lightweight construction is its relatively high strength with respect to its low density. The beech plywood used in the shell has a Young's modulus E of 17000 N/mm² and a density ρ of 730 kg/m³, resulting in a specific modulus of 23.3 (E/ρ). This is comparable to that of steel and roughly four times better than concrete while using only a fraction of the energy required to produce the specific building product. However, up until today, beech wood is rarely used in construction due to its susceptibility to warp in response to changing humidity.[2] Beech, however, plays a central role in future foresting strategies mainly due to its characteristic climate envelope that is aligned with Central Europe's expected climate in the coming decades (Kölling, 2007) and the proportion of harvested beech wood is expected to grow. The use of beech in the context of this project therefore provides the opportunity to reconsider its usage in architecture, not only in the light of foresting strategies, but also as a structural material that is particularly suited for lightweight construction. Consequently, the Landesgartenschau Exhibition Hall is one of the first buildings to use beech plywood as the main structural building material.

The use of regional materials, i.e. a decentralised production with short transportation routes from harvesting and processing of wood to fabrication and construction, contributes to timber architecture's unique potential for low embodied energy and, therefore, constituted a key premise in the construction of the shell. Effectively, this resulted in a radius of 200km around the site, within which all the wood used in the construction of the shell could be sourced: the beech wood used in the structural layer, the wood used in the fibre board insulation layer, and the larch wood used for the polygonal cladding panels (Figure 8.3). The project expands on the topic of regional resources in that the design, engineering and fabrication of the building all happened within a 100km radius of the site (Figure 8.4).[3] The project can therefore be a model for how timber construction can foster strong regional economic ties by feeding into a regional value chain: not only economically, but also ecologically and socially.

Construction and prefabrication

T HE three main layers of the shell, the structural beech layer, the insulation and water-proofing layer, and the final cladding layer, were each assembled on site in just one week respectively. Consisting of prefabricated components that have been shipped to the site directly

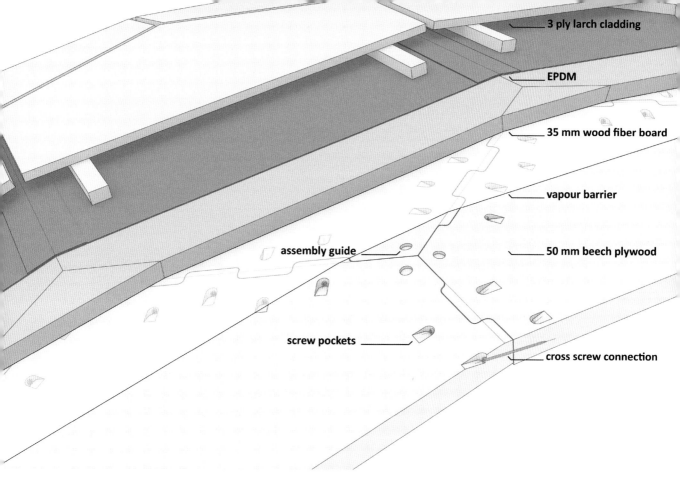

3 ply larch cladding

EPDM

35 mm wood fiber board

vapour barrier

50 mm beech plywood

assembly guide

screw pockets

cross screw connection

Figure 8.3
Construction layers of the shell.

from the workshop in a pre-defined assembly order, the entire shell was assembled over a temporary scaffold by only three workers in just under three weeks (Figure 8.5). With its relatively lightweight components and ease of transportation and handling, the timber plate system is ideally suited for prefabrication, and its associated benefits such as higher quality control and reduced construction times compared to labour intensive and high tolerance on-site fabrication are readily available. Additionally, within the controlled environment of the workshop, custom numerically controlled fabrication processes can be implemented on a project-by-project basis.

Figure 8.4
Locality of the material, design, and engineering.

Figure 8.5
Construction of the timber plate shell.

Process prototype

Fabrication and robotics

OPERATING at the intersection of research and practice, the researchers from the University of Stuttgart collocated at the timber fabricator's workshop where a mobile robotic milling cell was temporarily installed. This way, the robotic cell could be incorporated into an existing infrastructure and, in almost a plug-and-play fashion, a custom fabrication workflow could be implemented and tested in the real-world context of professional timber manufacturing. The workflow consisted of three consecutive steps, starting with (1) the pre-formatting of oversized plates on a CNC-controlled panel machine; at this step the plates, ranging in size from 960–2090mm diameter, were machined out of 2550 x 1850mm plywood plates and labelled, with the order being purely based on optimal material utilisation. The offcut generated in this step was used to cut lamellas for the parquet flooring, resulting in maximum usage of the employed wood resources. This was followed by (2) the milling of the intricate joint geometry including assembly details on a robotic milling cell, which consisted of a standard 6-axis industrial robot arm equipped with a spindle and an additional external axis as turn table (Figure 8.6). Finally, (3) sorting the finished parts into stacks based on assembly order concluded the fabrication stage of the structural plates (Figure 8.7). In parallel, all other elements of the multi-layered shell, including insulation,

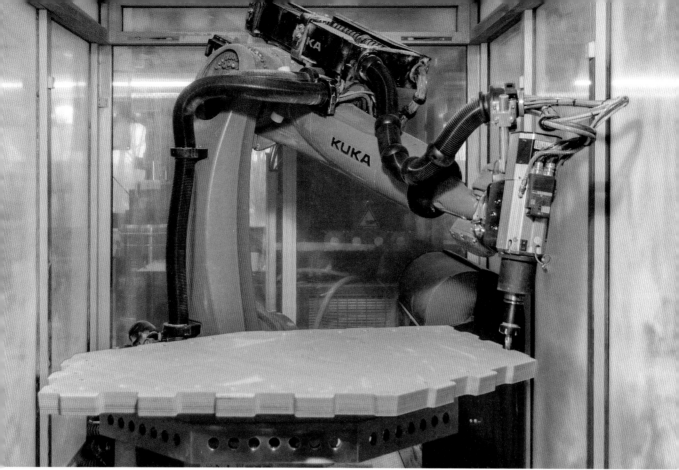

Figure 8.6

Robotic milling of the finger joints.

Figure 8.7

Sorted plates with close-up of joint details.

waterproofing, and cladding layers, could be digitally fabricated from the same digital information model and pre-assembled on the shop floor.

Joints and shells

THE structural layer of the shell consists of 243 geometrically unique beech plates that are edge-wise connected through a total of 7,356 individual finger joints. In shell structures, however, joints constitute the weak points as the stiffness continuity of the shell is interrupted (Li & Knippers, 2015). Therefore the design of shell structures traditionally aims at a continuity of the shell surface. This continuity is typically achieved through labour-intensive on-site construction of a full-scale formwork, on top of which the shell can be constructed, for example through pouring of concrete or layup of fibre mats in the case of fibre-composite shells. Such a process effectively requires the shell to be built twice, which seems neither resource- nor cost-effective and contradicts the potentially minimal material usage of the finished shell. While this might be the reason why continuous shell structures have become less common after a stage of experimentation in the 1950–1970s, segmented shells, on the other hand, consist of individual elements that can be prefabricated in the workshop and assembled on-site over simple scaffolding as demonstrated by the Landesgartenschau Exhibition Hall. Consequently, the research into segmented shells provides the opportunity to reconsider the economic and ecologic constraints of shell structures and re-take advantage of their structural and architectural benefits.

Since the load bearing capacity of the overall shell is largely dependent on the connections between the plates, a particular research focus was the further development of plate arrangement and the joint details based on previous research into biological role models for segmented shells (La Magna et al., 2013). The driving criterion for the further development was its relevance in the context of the building industry and meeting existing building code and regulations. Starting with material tests that informed Finite Element Modelling, a finger joint connection detail was developed, in which the main thrust of shear forces is transferred into the plane of the timber plate by the lateral contact surfaces between the joints. The much smaller axial and out-of-plane forces are accommodated by crossing screws (Figure 8.8). As the thin plates are to be connected edge-to-edge and the connection detail had to be integral to the plate, minimising material thickness but leaving enough material overlap as per building code for the screw connectors constituted a major challenge (Figure 8.9). On the other hand, the material overlap, which is a function of the shank diameter, also plays an important role in fire safety considerations as it provides insulation for the metal screw in the case of fire. These are just two of the conflicting goals that had to be negotiated in the design of plates and connections that ultimately resulted in plate thickness of 50mm. While this is slightly thicker than is required by structural calculations, plate thickness and joint design are ultimately not only based on structural considerations but also on aspects of building regulations, assembly on site and producibility (Krieg et al., 2015).

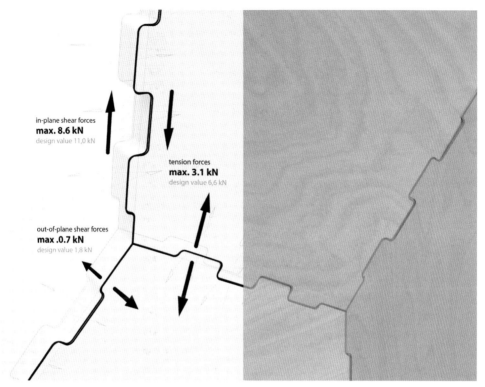

in-plane shear forces
max. 8.6 kN
design value 11,0 kN

tension forces
max. 3.1 kN
design value 6,6 kN

out-of-plane shear forces
max .0.7 kN
design value 1,8 kN

Figure 8.8
Force diagram of the plate–plate connection.

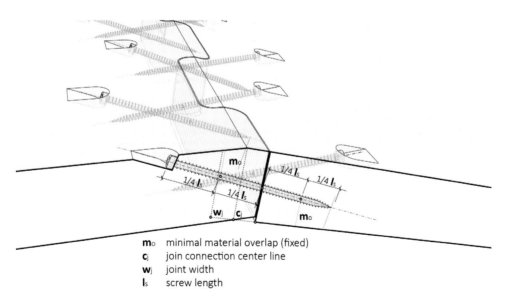

m_o minimal material overlap (fixed)
c_j join connection center line
w_j joint width
l_s screw length

Figure 8.9
Diagram of the joint detail including crossing screws.

FROM the point of view of applicability of a timber plate system in building practice the question of fabrication tolerances is particularly relevant. As there are no statements available regarding the accuracy of industrial robots in timber fabrication, a process for quality control was developed and implemented (Schmitt & Schwieger, 2015).

Tolerances in fabrication are usually accounted for in the joints between the elements by providing interstitial space in which inaccuracies of fabrication and assembly can be accommodated. On the other hand the structural integrity of the plate system demands an almost 'zero-tolerance' joint where adjacent teeth need contact in order to be able to transfer loads between the plates as previously discussed. This challenge is compounded by the material's susceptibility to warp under changing environmental conditions.

Therefore the purpose of quality control was two-fold: first to get an idea about a realistic accuracy in the robotic fabrication of the plates themselves; and second to investigate possible deformations of the plates between fabrication and assembly due to changing environmental conditions between workshop and building site. A laser-tracker with an accuracy of 5 μm over a distance of 10m and a custom-built measurement probe were used to establish a tracking process with an inherent accuracy of 0.11mm (Figure 8.10). Finally, by surveying 24 out of 243 plates, an in-plane, two-dimensional fabrication accuracy of 0.42mm could be calculated (Schmitt & Schwieger, 2015). This is an exceptionally low value given that tolerances in timber construction are usually measured in centimetres, and it fits well with the initial assumption of 0.5mm fabrication tolerances, for which the joints have been designed.

In addition, four plates were tracked a total of three times each in order to identify possible shape changes: immediately after fabrication, before delivery on site after storage, and before assembly into the shell. However, no statistically significant changes were recorded (Schmitt & Schwieger, 2015). This is an indication that the orthogonal lamination of the plywood cancelled out

Figure 8.10

Laser-tracking of plate edges to determine fabrication accuracy.

most of the three-dimensional shape changes and that the occasional slight warping of some plates did not significantly affect their in-plane accuracy which determines their ability to be assembled.

Design computation

Design integration and process

THE development of the Exhibition Hall aimed at integrating considerations regarding programme, geometry, assembly, fabrication, structure, joints, quality requirements, and building regulations. However, established design methods seem ill equipped to concurrently consider these sometimes conflicting requirements at an early stage in the process. Therefore a novel approach was explored within the context of this research that enables feedback between what are typically considered opposite ends of the planning spectrum. This requires an integrative process that goes beyond the statutory design and construction phases by integrating all stake-holders from the earliest design stages.

Design feedback and synthesis

IN order to enable such a process, the computational design environment plays a crucial role, as it is here where all the requirements are synthesised. This provokes the question, which computational design approaches are best suited to realise the necessary feedback and synthesis? In contrast to knowledge-based planning methods that encapsulate the knowledge of a specific domain, such as Building Information Modelling or Computer Aided Manufacturing, a behaviour-based approach was explored in this project using an agent-based modelling and simulation method (ABMS).

The method is inspired by the flocking behaviour of birds and schools of fish, in that each element of the flock – or plate system – calculates its position and orientation with respect to its immediate neighbours and the environment. Pre-defined but also flexible rules establish behavioural patterns, which, for example, control the distance of one agent to the next, thereby determining the size and shape of each plate in relation to the properties of the underlying double-curved surface (Schwinn, Krieg and Mendes, 2014). The intersection of a plane that is tangent to the surface at each agent's location with the ones of its neighbours consequently produces planar polygons that represent the individual outlines of the plates in the plate system (Figure 8.11).

The size of a producible plate is mostly dependent on the properties and extents of the available stock material as well as the constraints of the specific fabrication setup. These can be defined as a series of parameters that influence the behaviour of the agents in the autonomously controlled modelling and simulation process. In this way, it is possible to find solutions for conflicting design requirements. In contrast to methods of optimisation that require clearly defined

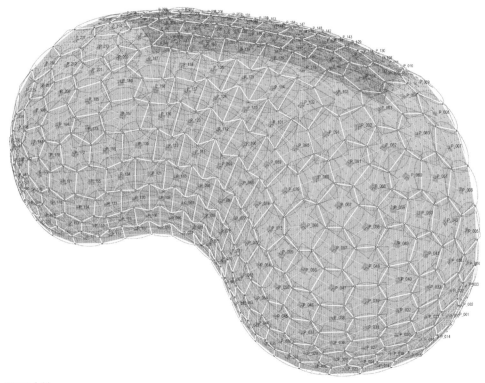

Figure 8.11
View of the agent model for plate systems.

objective functions, this process is explorative, such that it can search and find performative solutions to a combination of design requirements that include finding producible geometry within the solution space of the machine – its machinic morphospace (Menges, 2013).

Behaviour-based computational design

FINALLY, the proposed approach provides the possibility to be translated into a general method, which will be investigated in further research. On an abstract level, building elements can be considered n-dimensional points within an n-dimensional solution space that is defined by parameters of fabrication, assembly, joint design etc., as already outlined (Figure 8.12). Through the simultaneous representation as both 3-dimensional geometry and points within an n-dimensional solution space, agents can actively parse the design space and direct their movement across this space using behaviours that are defined by selected performance criteria (Schwinn & Menges, 2015). Compared to established processes, this completely changes the architectural design process and, by consequence, offers new and exciting opportunities for truly performative and sustainable architecture.

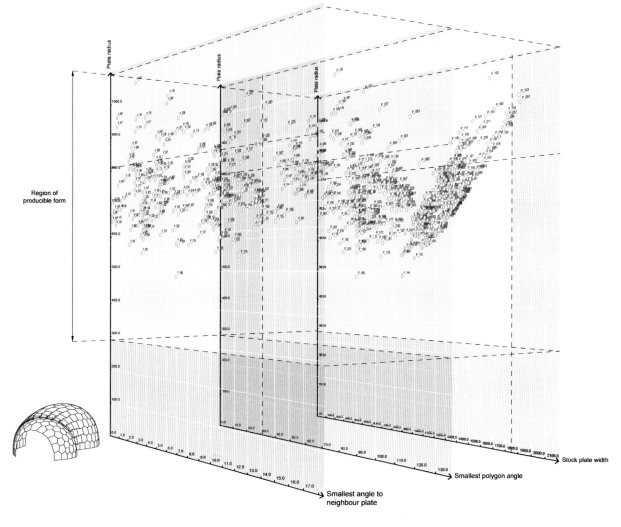

Figure 8.12
N-Dimensional machinic morphospace.

Acknowledgements

Tʜᴇ work presented in this paper was partially funded by the European Union through the European Fund for Regional Development (ERDF) and the state of Baden-Württemberg through the 'Clusterinitiative Forst und Holz' programme and was part of a joint research project between the University of Stuttgart and Müllerblaustein Holzbau GmbH involving Landesgartenschau Schwäbisch Gmünd 2014 GmbH, ForstBW and KUKA Roboter GmbH. The author would like to express his gratitude towards his colleagues Professor Achim Menges and Oliver David Krieg at the Institute for Computational Design, and fellow investigators, Professor Jan Knippers and Jian-Min Li at the Institute for Building Structures and Structural Design (ITKE), and Professor Volker Schwieger and Annette Schmitt at the Institute for Geodesic Engineering (IIGS), University of Stuttgart.

References

Kölling, C. (2007). Klimahüllen für 27 Waldbaumarten. *AFZ Der Wald*, 23, 1242–1245.

Krieg, O., Schwinn, T., Menges, A., Li, J., Knippers, J., Schmitt, A. & Schwieger, V. (2015). Biomimetic Lightweight Timber Plate Shells: Computational Integration of Robotic Fabrication, Architectural Geometry and Structural Design. In P. Block, J. Knippers, N.J. Mitra & W. Wang (eds), *Advances in Architectural Geometry 2014* (pp. 109–125). Cham: Springer.

La Magna, R., Gabler, M., Reichert, S., Schwinn, T., Waimer, F., Menges, A. & Knippers, J. (2013). From Nature to Fabrication: Biomimetic Design Principles for the Production of Complex Spatial Structures. *International Journal of Spatial Structures*, 28(01), 27–40.

Li, J.-M. & Knippers, J. (2015). Pattern and Form: Their Influence on Segmental Plate Shells. In *Proceedings of the International Association for Shell and Spatial Structures (IASS) Symposium 2015*. Amsterdam.

Menges, A. (2013). Morphospaces of Robotic Fabrication: From Theoretical Morphology to Design Computation and Digital Fabrication in Architecture. In S. Brell-Çokcan & J. Braumann (eds), *Rob/Arch 2012: Robotic Fabrication in Architecture, Art and Design* (pp. 28–47). Dordrecht: Springer.

Schmitt, A. & Schwieger, V. (2015). Quality Control of Robotics Made Timber Plates. In *FIG Working Week 2015*. Sofia, Bulgaria.

Schwinn, T., Krieg, O. & Menges, A. (2014). Behavioral Strategies: Synthesizing Design Computation and Robotic Fabrication of Lightweight Timber Plate Structures. In D. Gerber, A. Huang & J. Sanchez (eds), *ACADIA 2014: Design Agency Proceedings; Proceedings of the 34th Annual Conference of the Association for Computer Aided Design in Architecture, October 23–25, 2014, Los Angeles, California* (pp. 177–188).

Schwinn, T. & Menges, A. (2015). Fabrication Agency: Landesgartenschau Exhibition Hall. *Architectural Design*, 85(5), 92–99.

U.S. Green Building Council. (2015). Materials and Ressources: LEED v4 Building Design and Construction Guide. Retrieved from http://www.usgbc.org/guide/bdc.

Notes

1. See acknowledgments.
2. A parallel research endeavour that takes advantage of this phenomenon, which is the result of the hygroscopicity of the material, is presented in Chapter 9 by Oliver David Krieg.
3. For comparison, the LEED (Leadership in Energy and Environmental Design) certification system specifically credits materials sourced within a 160 km radius of the site (U.S. Green Building Council 2015). Materials sourced within an 800 km radius around the site are considered regional.

9

HygroSkin – Meteorosensitive Pavilion

Oliver David Krieg

Institute for Computational Design, University of Stuttgart, Germany

I N today's standardised production processes the idiosyncratic properties of wood, such as its elasticity, anisotropy, and hygroscopicity, are usually seen as deficiencies that are evened out in the manufacturing process of building products. In the project presented by Oliver David Krieg, research associate and doctoral candidate at the Institute for Computational Design at the University of Stuttgart, those properties are reconsidered and, instead, used as design drivers for the development of a novel, lightweight and modular timber construction system that takes advantage of wood's inherent material capacities. The reciprocal relation between material- and fabrication-oriented investigations forms the fundamental principle for the developed integrative architectural design approach – combining wood's elasticity and hygroscopicity with advanced robotic fabrication strategies that include as-built information into the prefabrication process. A particular innovation of this project is the first architectural application of a hygroscopically actuated façade system that obviates the need for electro-mechanical actuation by making intelligent use of the inherently available self-forming capacity of wood. The research ultimately proposes a low-tech solution to the complex requirements of adaptive façade systems where the material itself is the machine.

Introduction

A s a naturally grown building material, wood exhibits anisotropic behaviour as well as distinct structural characteristics unprecedented in its man-made counterparts. Computational design strategies and digital fabrication allow for the exploration of these material characteristics, and their utilisation in the design process. Instead of being seen as deficiencies in otherwise standardised production processes, wood's properties can become an active design driver in the development of new types of timber construction. The presented project is the result of ongoing research at the Institute of Computational Design into the differentiated material performance of wood and its reciprocities with computational design and digital fabrication methods. In the context of a full-scale architectural prototype, the research focused on lightweight timber construction methods as well as material-inherent, weather-responsive openings.

The HygroSkin – Meteorosensitive Pavilion project was commissioned by the FRAC Centre in Orléans, France, for its renowned permanent collection, and was first shown in the *ArchiLab 2013* exhibition. As a travelling pavilion the project development was subject to several constraints. For the purpose of transporting and storage, the pavilion was required to be a modular, lightweight, and self-supporting structure that would be easy to assemble and disassemble. These constraints necessitate a strategic use of material characteristics as well as fabrication technologies. The combination of both would enable the development of an effective and precise production process for a lightweight and stable construction system with a unique architectural appearance (Figure 9.1)

Strategic use of material characteristics

Wood: a high performance material

THE material behaviour of wood and its structural complexity derive from its cellular build-up as a naturally grown tissue. As evolution has driven wood to evolve specifically in order to meet the support, conduction and storage requirements of trees (Dinwoodie, 2000), accessing the material's complexity for its potential in today's design processes requires a reconceptualisation of architectural design in general (Correa et al., 2013). While many architects have become increasingly separated from intricate material characteristics and capacities (Kieran & Timberlake, 2004), current developments in computational design and fabrication enable a renewed and even deeper correlation between design, structure, material, and fabrication through a digital feedback in the development process. In order to unlock wood's inherent material performance on an architectural scale, the project's main goal was to develop a computational design and robotic fabrication strategy integrating both the elastic and the hygroscopic behaviour of wood as active drivers in the design process.

Material strategy: modular elastic bending

PREVIOUS research at the Institute for Computational Design explored how the elastic bending of wood enables the generation of complex, and structurally stable, geometries from initially flat sheets of plywood (Fleischmann et al., 2012; Krieg & Menges, 2013). The presented project continues this line of research and explores local elastic bending in the context of a modular construction system. The main area of interest is the utilisation of an underlying, developable bending geometry that can be used as a common denominator for differentiated module shapes

Figure 9.1 (facing page)

The HygroSkin – Meteorosensitive Pavilion as it was exhibited in the *ArchiLab 2013* exhibition.

through a repetitive and parametrically adaptive production process. In this context the geometry of a standard conical surface was of particular interest. Developable surfaces like the cone offer the opportunity to construct a geometrically stiff module from initially flat and elastic sheets.

Based on a common cone-like tapered surface a prefabrication process involving elastic bending was developed. While all modules are based on the same point-symmetrical cone, their individual boundary is the result of different partitions of that geometry (Figure 9.2a). When arranging multiple cones on a plane facing in the same direction, their resulting surfaces are defined by intersecting them with their neighbours (Figure 9.2b). These intersection curves define each cone's three-dimensional boundary and can yet be described as only single-curved. For fabrication purposes, the cone geometry can be unrolled into a flat sheet by introducing at least one seam from its centre to the edge, and thereby elastically bending the sheet (Figure 9.2c). The resulting single-curved connection between the modules (Figure 9.2d) is more resistant against lateral movement while simultaneously keeping the connection details simple. Additionally, only one formwork is needed to laminate the prefabricated sandwich modules with their differentiated outlines.

Since the module arrangement resembles that of a plate structure following the rule of not more than three elements meeting in one point (Schwinn, Krieg & Menges, 2014), the construction system naturally necessitates very low tolerances.[1] However, due to the cone modules' three-dimensional boundary the requirements in precision had to be met for both the modules' conical surface as well as its polygonal outline. In order to achieve such a level of precision the project development was driven towards a strategic use of available fabrication technology in conjunction with the material's elasticity and machinability.

Strategic use of fabrication technology

THE material's high elasticity and structural performance allow the use of only 4mm thin plywood for all elements of the developed construction system. With only three veneer layers the thinnest available plywood for building construction is considered ideal for the small bending radii close to the cone's centre point. The thin material is employed in a multi-material sandwich construction with an interior Styrofoam core. In order to ensure precision throughout the production the process is split into two steps making strategic use of the employed fabrication technology. First, vacuum forming is used to prefabricate raw module geometries exhibiting a precise cone surface. Afterwards, a robotic fabrication strategy is used to accurately trim each module to its required boundary.

In the first production step, Styrofoam strips are glued between two layers of elastically bent plywood under vacuum, combining them into one structural entity (Figure 9.3). Both layers of plywood have previously been cut out of flat sheets and bent into a cone surface by connecting their puzzle-jointed open edges. Vacuum pressure is applied onto the formwork until the glue is completely cured. This fabrication strategy allows the production of differentiated geometries for each module while using only one regularised formwork. Since all modules originate from the

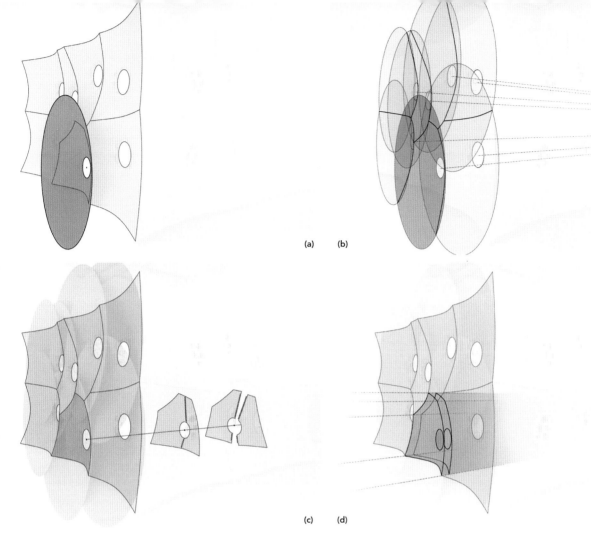

(a)   (b)

(c)   (d)

Figure 9.2

a) Each module is based on the same conical surface and is only differentiated through its specific boundary. b) When arranging multiple cones facing in the same direction their intersection defines the resulting surfaces. c) Since each module is based on a conical surface it can be produced through the elastic bending of initially flat sheets of plywood. d) In this particular case all modules' intersections and therefore their side faces are planar and single-curved.

same cone geometry, they can all be aligned with their centre points in order to determine their common geometric denominator, and thus the minimal formwork size (Figure 9.4).

While this first production step is feasible with common manufacturing techniques of low complexity, it is less useful for defining the exact module boundary. However, a highly precise formwork ensures low tolerances in the module's surface, which is a requirement for the subsequent production step. The formwork was therefore digitally fabricated and later evaluated through laser measuring techniques in order to analyse the relation between the formwork shape and the resulting module geometry. In a reference test the formwork and a prototype module were laser scanned, proving that the deviation from the computer-generated geometry was on average less than one millimetre (Figure 9.5). These findings were crucial since only a very

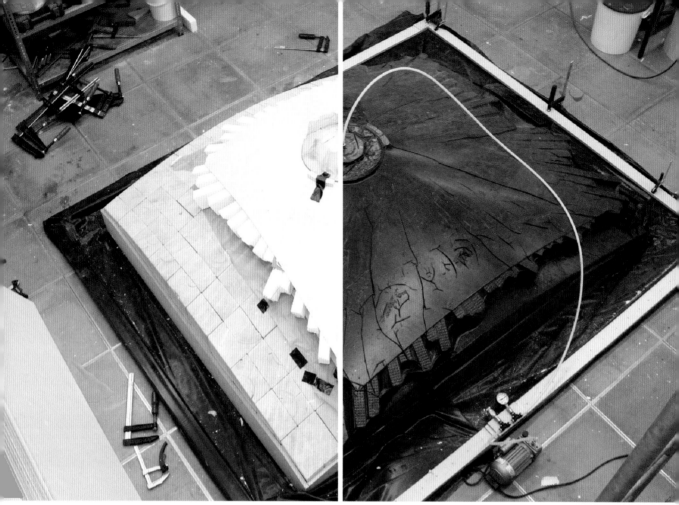

Figure 9.3
Each module is prefabricated by combining two outer plywood layers that are elastically bent to fit the cone shape and to include a Styrofoam core.

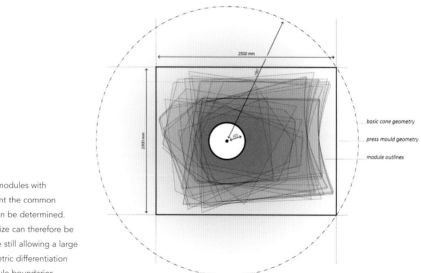

Figure 9.4
By aligning all modules with their centre point the common denominator can be determined. The formwork size can therefore be minimized while still allowing a large range of geometric differentiation within the module boundaries.

(a)

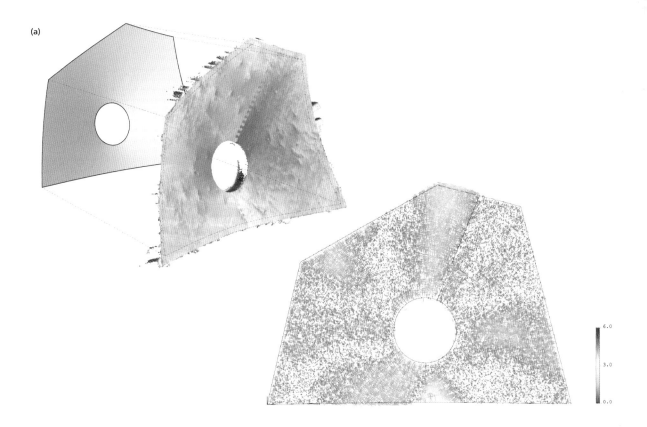

(b)

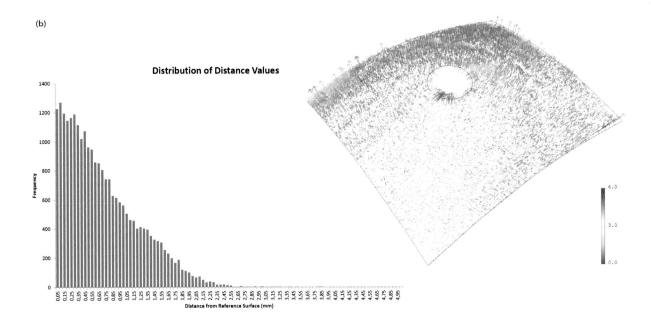

Figure 9.5

a) A prototype module is scanned and evaluated against the computer-generated geometry for its precision.

b) Also the formwork is scanned and evaluated. The deviation from the computer-generated model is shown in the graph.

high surface precision would allow for formatting the module's three-dimensional boundary in the second production step.

Compared to other projects involving robotic fabrication for timber processing, this project strategically employs an industrial robot not at the beginning of the process but as the last step. While previous projects profited from the robot's kinematic freedom and precision when processing raw material into building elements, they required additional, and mostly manual, labour before assembly on site. In this project, manual labour is employed effectively during the first production step, while the precise and complex movements required to trim the semi-finished modules to their exact boundary are executed by an industrial robot in the final step of production, where the highest accuracy is needed.

The modules are initially produced with an offset in order to allow tolerances when manually orienting them on the vacuum formwork. Once these semi-finished modules are placed on the robotic setup, the robot arm is used to survey their

Figure 9.6

a) The industrial robot is used to survey the prefabricated module's position on the turn table.
b) The fabrication data is then adjusted to the module's position.

exact position in relation to its own coordinate system in order to adapt the automatically generated fabrication data (Figure 9.6). The required level of precision can then be realised efficiently through two robotic fabrication steps: (1) using a saw blade for formatting the module outline, and (2) using a rasp milling tool for trimming the Styrofoam core inside (Figure 9.7).

The developed robotic fabrication technique significantly influences the construction system's design space, or morphospace, as it determines the producible module geometries in relation to the robot's kinematic freedom (Menges, 2013). The interrelation between the modules' possible geometric differentiation and fabrication parameters is a basic principle of an integrative architectural design approach. Ultimately, the construction system's design space is not only defined by the fabrication strategy, but also by transport, handling, and assembly constraints.

These constraints also influenced the overall assembly strategy. The modules are connected with standard slot and key joints, which lock neighbouring modules in place and also ensure a certain resistance against bending moments during the assembly process. The specific type of connection is characterized by constrained assembly directions. In combination with the polygonal module outlines, a predefined assembly sequence is required. At the same time, the assembly sequence influences which part of the connection (male or female) is used on which side of each module. Once finished, the designed shadow gaps between the modules make it easy to evaluate the precision of the construction system. As it was planned, the gaps were between 6 to 8mm even after reassembling the pavilion three times.

(b)

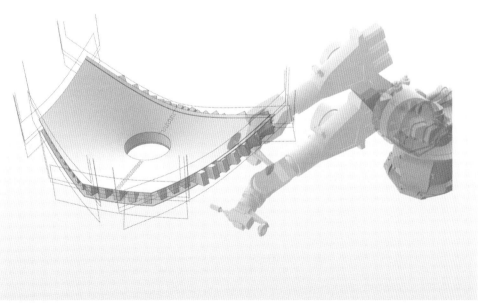

Figure 9.7

Two different fabrication steps are used to trim the semi-finished module to its exact boundary. The tool path is shown as dotted lines in the drawing. If its position had not been surveyed before the industrial robot would have cut out an unprecise shape.

One main characteristic of the cone geometry is an increasing curvature towards its centre. The minimum bending radius for the 4mm thin plywood exceeds this curvature at some point and would cause the plywood to fail. However, this constraint was used as an advantage during the design development for integrating another material-based innovation in the project. In the centre of each module, a hygroscopic aperture opens and closes with changes of relative humidity (Figure 9.8).

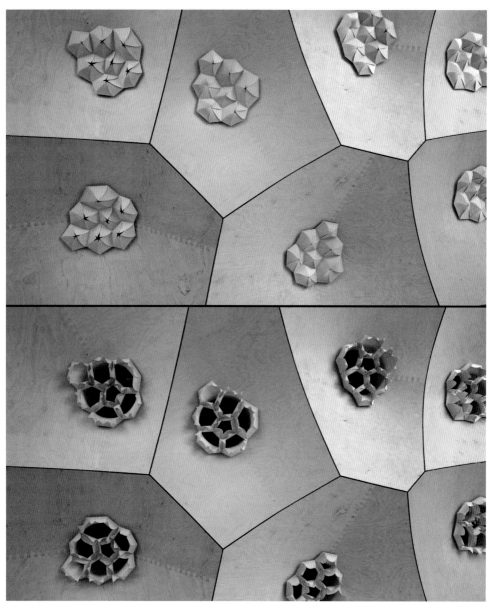

Figure 9.8

Each module of the HygroSkin Pavilion carries a hygroscopic aperture in its centre. The pro-programmed veneer closes with increasing relative humidity.

Integrated material performance

The cellular arrangements are a critical aspect for the hygroscopic characteristics of wood (Wagenführ, 1999). Changes in the surrounding relative humidity cause wood to expand and shrink unequally in the longitudinal, tangential, and radial direction to the fibres inside the tree trunk – a behaviour mostly seen as a disadvantage in wood working. However, in this project, the anisotropic dimensional instability of wood in relation to moisture content is employed to construct a weather-responsive architectural skin that autonomously opens and closes based on local weather changes. The same principle of moisture-related responsiveness can be found in the spruce cone, and it neither requires the supply of operational energy nor any kind of mechanical or electronic control.

Ongoing research in this field has been conducted at the Institute for Computational Design since 2008 (Reichert, Menges & Correa, 2015), and the latest findings were used in this project on an architectural scale and integrated into the modular construction system. For the hygroscopic actuation the veneer sheets are cut so that the actuation occurs perpendicular to the main fibre direction. In this particular project the material is programmed to close with increasing relative humidity. Each of the apertures are positioned as an oculus within the conical module. This configuration is both architecturally effective and functionally interdependent: the apertures are designed to fit in the area of the modules that would exhibit a bending radius too low for the 4mm plywood. Additionally, the concave conical shape of the modules provides shelter to the aperture units (Figure 9.9).

Figure 9.9
Close-up view of the pavilion. The substructure of the hygroscopic apertures follow the module's curvature.

Conclusion

THE design, prefabrication and assembly of this full-scale architectural prototype demonstrates how the strategic use of material characteristics and fabrication technology in the production process can support the development of an adaptive, lightweight and modular construction system. The project emphasises the necessity to strategically implement the newest fabrication technology such as industrial robots in order to take full advantage of their extended kinematic freedom. Additionally, the responsive behaviour of the apertures exhibits an opposite, low-tech solution to the complex requirements for adaptive façade systems. While relying fully on reversible material behaviour, it is integrated into the construction system and also serves to extend its functionality. On an architectural level, the module arrangement, the conical surfaces, and the

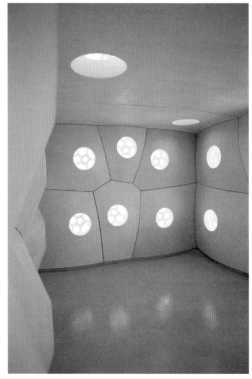

Figure 9.10

Interior view of the pavilion. The hygroscopic apertures are embedded in the conical modules and form a specific architectural articulation.

aperture's degree of opening form an intricate relation and a characteristic architectural articulation (Figure 9.10). Beyond fulfilling the functional requirements, the apertures' autonomous and passive actuation provides a unique interrelation between environmental and spatial experiences.

Acknowledgements

THE author would like to express his gratitude to the entire scientific development and robotic fabrication team of the HygroSkin project. This includes his colleagues Steffen Reichert, Nicola Burggraf, Zachary Christian, David Correa, Katja Rinderspacher, and Tobias Schwinn of the Institute for Computational Design, as well as Andreas Kulla and Edeltraud Walla of the Faculty Wood Workshop, and all participating students of the University of Stuttgart. The research in this article is based on Achim Menges' project commission of the HygroSkin Pavilion by the FRAC Centre in Orleans. Funding for this project was provided by the Fonds Régional d'Art Contemporain du Centre, as well as the Robert Bosch Stiftung, Cirp GmbH, Alfred Kiess GmbH, and Holzhandlung Wider GmbH.

References

Correa, D., Krieg, O., Menges, A., Reichert, S. & Rinderspacher, K. (2013). HygroSkin: A Prototype Project for the Development of a Constructional and Climate Responsive Architectural System Based on the Elastic and Hygroscopic Properties of Wood. In P. Beesley, M. Stacey & O. Khan (eds), *ACADIA 2013 Adaptive Architecture: Proceedings of the 33rd Annual Conference of the Association for Computer Aided Design in Architecture* (pp. 33–42). 24–26 October 2013, Cambridge.

Dinwoodie, J.M. (2000). *Timber, its Nature and Behaviour* (2nd edn). London, New York, England: CRC Press.

Fleischmann, M., Knippers, J., Lienhard, J., Menges, A. & Schleicher, S. (2012). Material Behaviour: Embedding Physical Properties in Computational Design Processes. *Architectural Design*, 82(2), 44–51.

Kieran, S. & Timberlake, J. (2004). *Refabricating Architecture: How Manufacturing Methodologies are Poised to Transform Building Construction*. New York, NY: McGraw-Hill.

Krieg, O. & Menges, A. (2013). Prototyping Robotic Production: Development of Elastically Bent Wood Plate Morphologies with Curved Finger Joint Seams. In C. Gengnagel, A. Kilian, J. Nembrini & F. Scheurer (eds), *Rethinking Prototyping: Proceedings of the Design Modelling Symposium Berlin 2013* (pp. 479–490). Berlin: Universität der Künste.

Menges, A. (2013). Morphospaces of Robotic Fabrication: From Theoretical Morphology to Design Computation and Digital Fabrication in Architecture. In S. Brell-Çokcan & J. Braumann (eds), *Rob/Arch 2012: Robotic Fabrication in Architecture, Art and Design* (pp. 28–47). Dordrecht: Springer.

Reichert, S., Menges, A. & Correa, D. (2015). Meteorosensitive Architecture: Biomimetic Building Skins Based on Materially Embedded and Hygroscopically Enabled Responsiveness. *CAD Journal*, 60, 50–69.

Schwinn, T., Krieg, O. & Menges, A. (2014). Behavioral Strategies: Synthesizing Design Computation and Robotic Fabrication of Lightweight Timber Plate Structures. In D. Gerber, A. Huang & J. Sanchez (eds), *ACADIA 2014: Design Agency Proceedings; Proceedings of the 34th Annual Conference of the Association for Computer Aided Design in Architecture, October 23–25 2014, Los Angeles, California* (pp. 177–188). Los Angeles: Acadia.

Wagenführ, R. (1999). Holz. Anatomie des Holzes: Strukturanalytik, Identifizierung, Nomenklatur, Mikrotechnologie (5th edn). Leinfelden-Echterdingen: DRW-Verlag.

Note

1. For detailed information on the geometric implications of plate structures see Chapter 8 by Tobias Schwinn.

PART FOUR

Design & Make Hooke Park, Architectural Association, England

10

Hooke Park
Applications for timber in its natural form

Martin Self

Architectural Association School of Architecture, England

Current and emerging digital technologies such as robotic fabrication and 3D-scanning of wood open up new opportunities to design, fabricate, and build with locally sourced, natural-form timber. Martin Self, director of the Architectural Association's Design & Make MArch programme, introduces ongoing research into the direct use of naturally curved and raw wood in prototypical buildings recently constructed and currently under construction at Hooke Park, the Architectural Association's woodland campus in the west of England. Hooke Park has a 30-year history of experimentation in wood architecture, including experimental structures conceived by Frei Otto in the 1980s, a tradition which is continued today through the building prototypes that are produced by students of the programme. Based on the premise that the grain structure of a particular piece of wood has evolved to enable maximum strength in response to the forces it was subjected to during growth, Martin Self outlines a research agenda that takes advantage of the specific local characteristics of timber: ranging from digitally cataloguing tree forms and applying Big Data strategies in order to match individual shapes contained in large databases and individual required joint geometries; to vision- and sensor-guided robotic machining that allows feedback between the material's anisotropic behaviour and the digital fabrication process not dissimilar to the hand-eye-touch coordination of the skilled human craftsman.

The paradoxes of engineered wood

The development of engineered wood products has contributed to recent advances in the application of wood in architecture by providing stable, consistent material that can be worked with in complex ways. However, this development leads to the paradox of wood being factory-processed into regularised products only to subsequently undergo complex subtractive digital fabrication processes to allow that material to be incorporated in geometrically complex organic building forms and structures. Furthermore, wood in its natural form consists of chains of cells – its grain fibres – that are optimally aligned to transmit force. Once these fibres are cut, the material immediately loses strength, meaning that most fabrication processes act to compromise the existing natural capacity of timber (Desch & Dinwoodie, 1996).

Of course, the benefits of engineered timber products such as laminated veneer lumber (LVL) and processes like glue-lamination are well known. By gluing veneers or laminas together, mechanical consistency and stability can be achieved which is only possible in un-processed wood through intimate craftsman-like knowledge of the behaviour of a given species. Engineered products remove or even-out the 'flaws' in timber, such as knots, producing predictability. However, this homogenisation of the wood also, arguably, acts to reduce the specific characteristic qualities of timber and reduces it to generic 'stuff' that can be used without really understanding the true, microscopic, living anatomy of the material. The risk is that wood is perceived primarily as a means to achieve shape, rather than as a complex material with specific properties that can be best exploited by understanding its idiosyncrasies rather that averaging them out.

A second paradox inherent in the use of industrially produced engineered wood products comes as a consequence of the tendency towards centralisation of their manufacture. The resultant embodied energy of transportation and processing compromises wood's unique environmental credentials. Economic forces encourage standardisation and mass-production, and favour consistency of raw material and thus a forestry mono-culture. This is counter to the tendency – in the UK at least – towards forests becoming more diverse rather than less (Ray, Morison and Broadmeadow, 2010), a trend that is necessitated by the need to increase robustness against both climate change and disease. This is amplified by the fact that timber as a material is produced almost anywhere, whereas for example steel production requires a centralised infrastructure. Hence an alternative view of a distributed, localised model of timber production for architecture is seen as more sympathetic to the realities of wood and requiring less energy input.

Reflecting the principles of the maker movement and of dispersed manufacturing, enabled by new low-cost manufacturing and communication technologies, a model of locally focused forestry, processing, new fabrication and construction becomes compelling.

Hooke Park

Hooke Park represents these issues in microcosm (Figure 10.1). It is a 150-hectare woodland in the west of England that is owned by the London-based Architectural Association (AA). It is used for architecture students to pursue design research in timber and to test this research in actual buildings realised on the campus within the forest. Resources include the trees themselves (a mix of broadleaf and conifer species) as well as sawmilling and workshop facilities, which means that the immediate sourcing of building material can be integrated within design. This

Figure 10.1 (facing page)
Aerial view of Hooke Park, May 2014.

agenda was inherited from the Parnham School of Woodland Industries when the AA took over the site in 2002. Led by furniture designer John Makepeace, the Parnham School had completed three buildings at the campus which themselves are demonstrators of novel approaches to using roundwood sources from the immediately surrounding woodland (Dickson & Parker, 2014).

Conceived initially by Frei Otto and designed with architects Ahrends Burton Koralek, the Hooke Park Prototype House and Workshop both use small-diameter spruce (*Picea abies*) thinnings to carry axial forces within their structures. The Prototype House (1987) (Figure 10.2) consists of a tent-like enclosure, of which the roof is formed by spruce elements in tension. For the end connections of these elements, a conical epoxy-plug connection was developed with engineers Buro Happold, creating full capacity tension connections that allow fully exploiting the remarkable tension strength of timber. Conversely, the Workshop (Figure 10.3) deploys spruce thinnings in a series of compression arches that act together to form a three-bayed shell structure. In both cases, timber that was initially straight has been elastically bent into the required curved structural forms, such that the catenary load paths of axial force follow the timber direction and thus the grain direction. Leaving the wood 'in-the-round' meant that the full natural axial capacity is maintained, as all of the grain fibrils remain intact (Burton, Dickson, & Harris, 2010).

The Westminster Lodge student dormitory building (1995) also uses small-diameter spruce thinnings, in this case to form a gently domed turfed roof. Arranged in a two-way spanning lattice grid, the green roundwood thinnings were spliced to form long elements that span the central 9x9m communal space and over sail the eight surrounding bedrooms. As with the earlier

Figure 10.2

The Hooke Park Prototype House (1985) demonstrated the use of roundwood timber thinnings in tension.

buildings, the dormitory was constructed using raw material from immediately surrounding forestry activity, and using small-scale tools in combination with new technologies. As such, each building demonstrates the potential for the application of local material in sympathy with small-scale forest maintenance.

In 2002, the AA took ownership of Hooke Park and began to develop teaching programmes there. For example, from 2005 to 2009 the Hooke Park workshop facility was used to fabricate a series of experimental timber pavilions driven by digital design and fabrication techniques. Tutored by Charles Walker and Martin Self, and using the London Serpentine Gallery pavilion programme as a precedent (the tutors had worked on the pavilions at Arup, including the robot-fabricated 2005 timber pavilion by architects Alvaro Siza and Eduardo Souta de Moura), student teams conceived, designed and fabricated structures that were exhibited outside the AA in London each summer. Through these projects, a series of investigations were carried out into the marriage of laminated-veneer-lumber and the digital design and fabrication tools at Hooke Park. The research included fractal branching structures, CNC-cut doubly curved glue laminated beams, and other methods of deriving complex geometric forms from flat-sheet material (Self & Walker, 2010) (Figure 10.4).

Figure 10.3

Hooke Park's Workshop (1989) during construction. Here locally sourced roundwood is deployed in a compression structure.

These pavilion projects developed a skill-base at Hooke Park in CNC machining, but were wholly detached from the immediate material resource at Hooke Park. The irony of using material made of spruce trees shipped from Finland in a workshop surrounded by spruce trees (and indeed built from those spruce trees) resulted in the intent to return to the original philosophy of the Parnham College and concentrate on the use of local timber. This led to the idea of combining the use of locally sourced material with the potential of new digital design and fabrication technologies as tested through the pavilion programme.

Design & Make

THE opportunity to implement this came in 2010, with the update of an extant planning permission (and associated donor funding) to create a new masterplan for growth of the Hooke Park campus. Sixteen new buildings were proposed, each of which would become vehicles for student design-build research in the AA's Design & Make MSc programme. Students conceive,

Figure 10.4
The Driftwood Pavilion (2009) by AA Intermediate Unit 2.
Photo: Valerie Bennett

detail and construct buildings on a 16-month cycle, contributing to an on-going programme of anticipatory design research underlined by the premise that architectural propositions are best tested through their realisation.

The first project was a large assembly workshop (the 'Big Shed', Figure 10.5) constructed from roundwood larch (*Larix spp.*) thinnings that would house future fabrication activities. Aiming to continue the inherited philosophy of using raw timber from the surrounding woodland, but acknowledging that the woodland had aged (and hence was no longer a source of the small diameter trees used in the bent-wood structures of the 1980s), here large irregular trusses were fabricated from unregularised roundwood larch poles using engineered woodscrews for the node connections. The trusses form portal frames, between which a series of triangle facets form the envelope. These are clad using corrugated steel for the roof and western red cedar (*Thuja placata*) from the Hooke Park woodland for the walls. The building now houses the robotic arm fabrication facility as well as open space for general prototyping and timber framing activities.

Following the completion of the assembly workshop, three small houses were completed at the site, each of which has tested aspects of using timber from the Hooke Park woodland in their structures and fit out. Whilst not structurally innovative as such, the projects have seen students test a variety of wood species in different applications. For example self-built bespoke window frames in sweet chestnut (*Castanea sativa*) allowed a student accommodation lodge to be designed around a set of re-claimed double-glazed window units (Figure 10.6). Western red cedar has been

Figure 10.5
The 'Big Shed' Assembly Workshop (2012) by AA Design & Make with Mitchell Taylor Workshop and Atelier One.
Photo: Valerie Bennett

used for cladding in various formats, and both beech (*Fagus sylvetica*) and poplar (*Populus spp.*) from the woodland have been used for flooring and other interior components. These exercises have added to the tacit knowledge held by the students and tutors about the individual characteristics of each species in different applications.

The Timber Seasoning Shelter (2014) (Figure 10.7) and Biomass Boiler House (2015) (Figure 10.8) projects developed alternative and opposing strategies for creating architectural geometries without the need for subtractive machining that tends to compromise the natural grain fibres. As an extension to the techniques used in the three original Hooke Park buildings (in which elastic bending was used to generate curvature of their timber elements), the student designers of Timber Seasoning Shelter applied steam bending processes to plastically deform timber. Parallel-grain straight planks were cut from beech trees and then steam bent to form pairs of elements that function as short trusses within the global three-direction reciprocal structure. Because the curved elements have been plastically curved from initially straight planks through steam-bending, the grain fibres were kept intact and simply re-aligned to the required structure form. This was achieved without machining or gluing.

Figure 10.6
The South Lodge.

Figure 10.7 (below)
The Timber Seasoning Shelter.

Figure 10.8
The Biomass Boiler House.

Curvatures in the Boiler House were formed using an opposite approach: by using naturally curved trees. Rather than manipulating straight timber into curves, here a naturally formed curvature was exploited directly by using Douglas fir (*Pseudotsuga Menzisii*) that had grown with basal sweeps. By stacking them in a manner similar to traditional log cabin construction, the key strategy was to digitally 3D-scan all the standing trees and then compose a flowing curved wall from a database of geometries of all those trees. The project hints at a radical opportunity presented by re-thinking the potential of natural geometry in timber. The 3D scanner used for the Boiler House project – the Kinect sensor from the Microsoft XBox gaming system – is cheap, and the geometric data it produces is relatively easy to manipulate. Therefore it is speculated that there will be a return to the traditional consideration of timber, in which natural grown form has particular value, as opposed to the current situation where straight trees have the greatest value, as they can be processed by centralised industrialised sawmills and producers.

Natural form

The deliberate sourcing of curved timber reflects the sophisticated structural use of curved oak branches in English and French warship-building in the seventeenth century (Matthew, 1831). The very specific geometric and structural requirements for different components of the ship were matched to the naturally grown tree (Figure 10.9). Motivated by the desire for naval power, trees were nurtured and surveyed to maximise the availability of timber of particular curved shapes, such as 'crooks' and 'knees'. To give an idea of quantity, a 1608 survey of southern England's New Forest identified 124,000 trees suitable for use in warship construction.[1] One can imagine a future version of that survey, with self-navigating UAVs mounted with 3D-scanners autonomously surveying every tree in woodlands to collate large digitised catalogues of tree geometries. In that scenario, designers and fabricators could use those catalogues to have access to a choice of thousands of naturally grown curved timber elements.

An associated axis of research at Hooke Park concerns the use of naturally formed wood joints in construction. The premise here is that the grain structure of a branching joint within a tree has evolved so as to produce maximum strength in resistance to the particular forces it is subjected to. Usually it is the connection sizing that governs the required cross-section for structural timber elements. In other words, timber elements have to be oversized to accommodate the components that transfer forces from one piece of timber to another. This is because of the specific anisotropic nature of timber and the difficultly in transferring forces out of one set of grain fibres and into another. However if the loading condition within a structure matches the forces that a component was subjected to when it was part of a tree, it will have a grain arrangement that is pre-optimised as a structural joint. Recent X-ray tomography studies of the anatomy of wood forks have shown highly complex interlocking grain patterns that strengthen the wood in that area (Slater & Ennos, 2015).

It is therefore proposed to develop techniques that allow naturally formed joints to be deployed in structures, and in particular to use 3D-scanning and form-finding techniques to configure these branching components within optimised topologies. By 'shuffling' between

Figure 10.9

Plate 103 from the *Encyclopédie Méthodique: Marine* (1798) illustrating the sourcing of natural-form timber elements for shipbuilding.

available component geometries (for example drawn from the large database of 3D-scanned trees) and using an equilibrium method to optimally align elements, a process is conceived in which natural tree junctions can be reconfigured into architectural structures (trusses, domes, space-frames) without needing complex connection hardware. Such an approach is being explored in a woodchip storage barn that Design & Make students plan to realise in late 2015 (Figures 10.10 and 10.11). A large-span Vierendeel truss formed from a chain of large beech forks is proposed in which the fork junctions contribute bending stiffness to the truss.

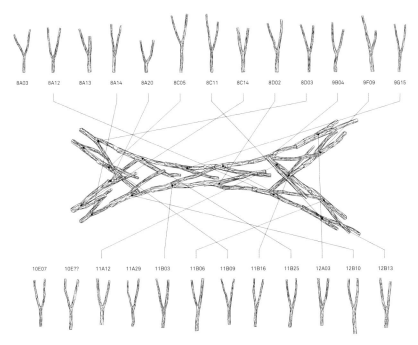

Figure 10.10

Placement of tree-fork components for the proposed Woodchip Barn structure. An evolutionary optimisation procedure determines component positions within the truss according to structural criteria.

Image: Zachary Mollica

Figure 10.11

Model of the proposed structure for the Woodchip Barn.

Image: Mohaimeen Islam

Robotic fabrication and feedback

THE rise of the use of robotics in timber fabrication and other architectural applications also gives new value to raw, natural-form timber. A generic industrial robotic arm need not be limited to processing straight, sawn, timber like conventional high-end timber fabrication machinery, and so has more freedom to operate on raw natural geometry. The recently installed 6-axis robot arm at Hooke Park is being set up to allow direct machining of roundwood and naturally formed curved and forked timber. A lathe-like arrangement, with timber elements carried horizontally on a controlled seventh rotational axis, is currently being tested. Traditional timber framing techniques – such as 'snapping' projected centrelines with string and 'scribing' the setting out of connection joinery – are still relevant and are being replicated within the workflow. And again, integrating with 3D scanning technologies will allow for direct feedback between the existing natural and fabricated forms. Real-time scanning of the position of the irregular raw timber surface could be fed back into the software generating the robot's tool path, so as to optimise that tool path.

This feedback could be extended. A vision system could map grain patterns during machining and, in real-time, adjust the machined geometry accordingly. Or the force generated between the machining tool and the wood component could be monitored using load-cells and used to adjust machining feed-rates and directions. Ultimately, this tends towards the full replication of a craftsman-like approach, digitally simulating the human's ability to feed information from the senses of vision and touch back to the tool; that is the hand-eye-touch coordination of the skilled carpenter. And whilst not falling into the trap of imagining that the holistic intuitive capabilities of the skilled human craftsman can (or should be) recreated by the machine, it does seem clear that these technologies will act to enrich the roles that timber, in all of its forms, can play in architecture.

To return to the global argument, wood has essential importance in the future of architecture given its environmental credentials compared to other industrialised building materials. This chapter has proposed that wood has fundamental differences to those other materials, because it grows both ubiquitously and with specific local characteristics. These characteristics should be exploited and celebrated, and with new technologies, it is entirely possible to grow, harvest, fabricate and build with local timber in sophisticated and as-yet unimagined ways.

References

Burton, R., Dickson, M. & Harris, R. (2010). The Use of Roundwood Thinnings in Buildings: A Case Study. *Building Research & Information*, 26(2), 76–93.

Desch, H.E. & Dinwoodie, J.M. (1996). *Timber: Structure, Properties, Conversion and Use* (7th edn, rev.). New York: Food Products Press.

Dickson, M. & Parker, D. (2014). *Sustainable Timber Design*. Hoboken: Taylor and Francis.

Matthew, P. (1831). *On Naval Timber and Arboriculture*. Neil & Co. Printers.

Ray, D., Morison J. & Broadmeadow, M. (2010). Climate Change: Impacts and Adaptations in England's Woodlands. Forestry Commission Research Note.

Self, M. & Walker, C. (eds) (2011). *Making Pavilions: AA Intermediate Unit 2, 2004–09*. AA Agendas/Architectural Association London: Vol. 9. London: AA Publications.

Slater, D. & Ennos, R. (2015). Interlocking Wood Grain Patterns Provide Improved Wood Strength Properties in Forks of Hazel (*Corylus avellana L.*). *Arboricultural Journal*, 37(1), 21–32.

Note

1. Referenced in *The Journal of the House of Commons* 47, 1792.

11

The Timber Seasoning Shelter at Hooke Park

Glen Stellmacher

Architectural Association School of Architecture, England

Oₙₑ of the most relevant characteristics of timber constructions is its potential for a negative carbon foot print, effectively storing more CO_2 in the structure than is released into the atmosphere during its fabrication and construction. This potential hinges on the availability of locally sourced wood, minimizing the need for transportation, and the low level of energy consumption during its processing. In an increasingly fast-paced building industry, however, lumber is usually kiln-dried, thereby compromising timber construction's potentially outstanding carbon footprint. Glen Stellmacher, graduate of the University of Washington and the Architectural Association's Design & Make programme, introduces the Timber Seasoning Shelter at Hooke Park, Dorset (UK), an agricultural structure whose ambition is not only to use locally sourced, under-utilized beech wood, but also to use it in its green state. Through physical experimentation, mock-ups and mechanical testing, the building's design and its custom manufacturing process have been developed concurrently. The result is a unique structure that synthesizes local materials, manufacturing, and architectural design, thereby forcing us to reconsider the architectural value and possibilities of locally available but possibly under-rated resources.

Abstract

Tₕₑ timber seasoning shelter at Hooke Park is the result of a body of material research and experimentation executed by four students of the Architectural Association Design & Make Master of Architecture programme. The building serves a function as an agricultural structure for the storage of raw materials, but also represents the continuation of an ethos of experimental architecture at Hooke Park. The primary driver of the design process combines computational design and fabrication with the inherent structural and manipulable potentials of locally sourced materials. The utilization of local, seemingly low value resources in an innovative manner was a common goal by all involved, across the disciplines of architecture, engineering, education, and forestry. The process of steam bending was conducive to achieving these goals and was coupled with the use of European beech as a building timber. Physical experimentation, proof of concept mock-ups, and mechanical testing were employed to prototype connections, formal arrangements, manufacturing processes, and material behaviour. The architecture is an artefact of prototypical approaches towards local materials, manufacturing, and design.

Introduction

THE timber seasoning shelter is a building at Hooke Park, serving as a shelter for the storage and seasoning of raw materials processed and harvested on site (Figures 11.1 and 11.2). Completed in 2014, it is located below a steep hill on the northern edge of the working yard area. The arrangement of the building parallels the contours of the site, interlocking with the base of a small hill (Figure 11.3). The team's intention was to place the building in a position which was easily accessible to forestry equipment, adjacent to the main entrance road to the campus. It is a simple building, with three timber storage bays that open to the southwest to facilitate unobstructed airflow through the timber stacks. Concrete ground beams and steel piles support canted columns, accommodating for the overall bracing of the structure. These columns support the timber roof of reciprocal, steam-bent components.[1] A highly translucent PVC-coated polyester membrane is used as a covering, resulting in a light and delicate canopy structure. The project was completed as part of the Architectural Association's Design & Make (MArch) course. Four students, along with a team of supporters, used the design, fabrication, and construction of the project as the principal output of their degree.

Beyond being an addition to the campus' infrastructure, the building represents the physical outcome of a research agenda spanning 12 months. The simplicity of the brief (to design a shelter) allowed exploration of the potentials of raw, underutilized grown material that can be harvested on site at Hooke Park. The team desired to reappraise the traditional technique of steam bending at the scale of a building,

Figure 11.1

The Timber Seasoning Shelter at Hooke Park.

Figure 11.2
The Timber Seasoning Shelter at Hooke Park.

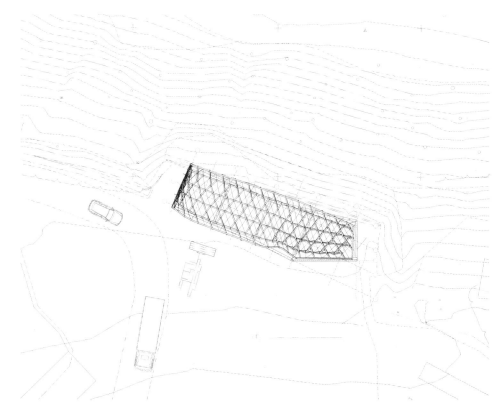

Figure 11.3
The Timber Seasoning Shelter protects 150m² of covered area for the air seasoning of locally sawn timber from Hooke Park.

in a contemporary manner. This agenda encompassed collaborative goals and an economy of means. The building is informed and conceived as a product of its environment; the potentials of a single local material are the starting point for an intensive empirical and scientific plan for its improved use.

Material methodologies

THE material, European beech, is rarely, if ever, used as a building timber. Its pre-war importance as a material for household goods and furniture made it a high value timber, too expensive for the building trade. However, in today's market, beech's use in household items has been supplanted by plastics, leaving the material as a low value timber. Beech stands in great abundance at Hooke Park, where it covers 27% of the woodland. However, once thinned, the material has little value in its primary market of fuel wood (one cubic meter of beech sells for £45). The team's first goal was to find a way to use this abundant low value resource in a smarter way. In literature, beech is stronger than European oak.[2] Also, its historic use in furniture took advantage of its excellent bending properties. This warranted a reappraisal of the material as a building resource.

The desire to specifically target beech as the primary building material arose from the ethos of previous construction at Hooke Park. The Workshop and Refectory utilized forest resources which were considered as waste products at the time. The resultant architecture from this approach is structurally innovative, spatially intricate, and acts to make the socio-economic and environmental opportunities of forestry into opportunities for architecture (Figure 11.4). These buildings are extremely successful case studies for sustainable and enduring built innovation. Perusing the historical archives of all projects at Hooke Park

Figure 11.4

The thinning of beech at Hooke Park took place over the span of two months. These trees were then utilized in the construction of the Timber Seasoning Shelter.

began to instil a sense of common purpose, transcending time, in the hope of better utilizing our natural resources, deriving form from their potentials. Andy Goldsworthy's theory behind the Hooke Park entrance gates (since demolished in 2015) remains key to the enduring ethos of the place. He wrote, 'I had some idea of the form, but left the scale and nature of the work to be resolved in the making. I wanted the form to come out of the material and place' (Goldsworthy, 1987) Designing within this context motivated the team to pursue a similar ideology, however, set within contemporary imperatives. The continued success and expansion of Hooke Park is indicative of the successful potential of these ideologies to foster a vibrant community, concomitant with exciting experimental architecture.

In the beginning of the project, much time was invested in researching beech before making the decision to pursue its use. Beech's durability classification as 'susceptible' to decay was potentially problematic (British Standard, 1994). Historical research drove the design and engineering teams to challenge the contemporary classification of beech's durability. Simultaneously, along with research on durability, came research on beech's uses. Throughout history it has been prolifically used in steam bent furniture, leading the design team to investigate the process of steam bending. This process was driven by ideals in the economic use of material to its maximum potential, aligning closely with the design goals at Hooke Park.

A confluence of factors resulted in the use of the steam bending technique at a building scale. For one, the shelter was required to cover a span of 6m of rough sawn stacks of lumber. Since the foresters at Hooke Park were not able to source lengths of timber this long from beech, the design team was challenged to cover this span with lumber sized consistently between 2 and 3.5 metres in length. The team opted for investigating reciprocal grillages, which collectively span larger distances than the lengths of each individual member of the system. Typically, these systems are connected through sophisticated joinery, or subtractive machining processes. Manipulating the material by steam-bending would allow the use of a thin section of material and a simple planar connection, as opposed to machining at each joint. The process also influenced the global design through the aggregated changes of many components over a given distance. Additionally, moulded steam-bending gave each component an efficient truss shape. Thus, the technique of steam bending was advantageous at the building scale.

A tactile understanding of the limitations of the steam-bending process through physical prototypes, mock-ups and testing was vital to the completion of the project. Without this haptic knowledge, surely, a less inspiring result would have emerged. The requirements for each member were to be easily bendable while still being structurally sufficient. Explorations with physical prototypes allowed for a greater understanding of the material properties and the subtleties of bending large sections of solid hardwood (Figure 11.5). Gradually, the design of the beech member size arrived at a thickness of 35mm and a width of 140mm. Although the member thickness and joint connections remained consistent throughout the structure, the component geometries were unique due to the parametric nature of the project. This allowed the team to make real time adjustments of component lengths to match material thinned from the forest, taking matrices of timber calculations into parametric software to corroborate the lengths of the pieces digitally. As a result, a large portion of the timber that was felled and diverted to the project could be utilized.

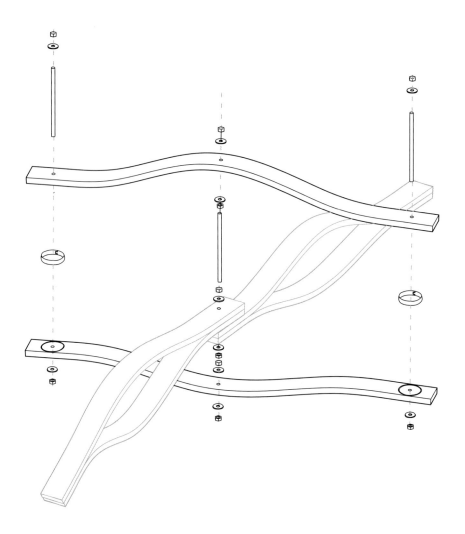

Figure 11.5

Within the reciprocal structural system, two components meet, and are supported by a third component. Each component is fitted with a split ring to accommodate for the high sheer stresses within each end.

Each unique component is defined from the lofting of a physical spline in space on a lofting floor. Dimensions from a drafted centreline to the spline are taken and defined as a table of offsets. That table of dimensions is then used to offset the components from a digital surface, reinterpreting an intersection of the surface as a unique centreline each time. This creates the flat, planar connection at each joint, and maintains the structural depth required of the components themselves as they negotiate subtle changes through space.

Structural resolution

PARAMETRIC tools allowed for a unique method of manufacturing the timber components. A standard office projector was used to project the shapes at full scale onto a bending jig (Figure 11.6). Digital scripts allowed the user to select at any moment the component they wished to manufacture. The projection was then utilized as a template, and adjustable blocking was secured in position along the curvature. The components were steamed for 90 minutes each, then placed in the jig and pressed into the adjustable formwork by an array of pneumatic rams. Each component was manufactured as a pair, temporarily fixed together and removed from the bending jig to set overnight. A similar process of projection onto a table-top jig was utilized at a secondary process called the assembly table. Here, to match the digitally prescribed shape as closely as possible, any warpage or shape distortion was corrected using clamps and shims. Once matching the prescribed shape on the assembly table, the bolt holes were drilled using a specially fabricated horizontal drilling machine. These holes were then used to register the split ring grooves into each component in the correct location. Once fastened together with split-ring

Figure 11.6

The bending jig utilizes two arrays of pneumatically actuated rams to press the steamed timber into an adjustable formwork. The rams are actuated from a control panel immediately adjacent to the computer, which controls the desired digital projection. The assembly table can be seen in the background.

connectors at each end, the shapes avoided radical distortion or relaxation into flat planks and remained relatively stable.

However, due to the fast-paced nature of the Design & Maker course, there was little time to season the material felled for the project. The most effective moisture content depends on the size of the material and the process in which it will equalize with its environment. For the timber seasoning shelter, bending beech at a moisture content of 20–25% was deemed optimal, but the available wood that the team ended up using had moisture contents in the range of 50–70%. Material that has a higher moisture content takes longer to equalize with the environment, and is susceptible to checking, while material with a lower moisture content is susceptible to tension failure in the steam bending process.

While the utilization of green timber saves an enormous amount of energy compared to kiln treated lumber,[3] it also proved problematic. Assembly became difficult due to the warped, shrunk or misshapen components after their processing through the bending jig, especially in areas of complex or tight curvature, where seamless assembly of the components relied heavily on the accuracy of the pieces. During the process of steam-bending at the furniture scale, a bending jig is used to bend the piece, and then the piece is transferred to a drying jig, where it is allowed to equalize its moisture content with the environment. The piece is then 'set firm' in the drying jig typically after days of rest depending on its internal moisture content and the thickness of the section. The team at Hooke Park was not able to produce unique, disposable drying jigs for each component, and therefore opted for a strategy to treat the structure itself as a drying jig. As soon as the components were assembled, they were used to construct four large roof sections (approximately 10x10m) in the assembly workshop (Figure 11.7). This positioned the components at their correct location within the structure, and minimized any further deformation through the rigidity and interconnection of the reciprocal structural system. The relationship between the utilization of 'green' sawn lumber and the notions of precision and tolerance within advancing digital processes are far from resolved within this project. The mitigation or exploitation of movement and shrinkage is part of the challenge and opportunity in integrating contemporary digital methods of design with the use of raw materials.

Because of the changing moisture content and alteration of the chemical and physical structure of the wood after steam-bending, significant proof of concept structural testing was undertaken by the team. In-house density testing confirmed the properties of the timber into class D30 of the British building standards, a high strength deciduous lumber classification.[4] Team partners at Bath University administered flexure and compressive testing on steamed and un-steamed samples provided from Hooke Park. ARUP then utilized these findings to study the behaviour of the components digitally, using graphic statics software. With vestigial feelings of uncertainty in the material behaviour, a handful of components were required to be stress tested to full design loads before installation into the large swatches of roof. These components were highly stressed, some receiving up to 40kN of load through their central axis. An ad-hoc testing rig was developed and implemented to assure the components satisfied these structural requirements before installation. Occasionally, the 35mm sections were too slender for the design loads, and in these instances, plywood 'web stiffeners' were added. These stiffeners were only added

Figure 11.7

Component fabrication required many stages before construction into the large prefabricated swatches of structure. The operations included the bending jig (top left), assembly table (top middle), load testing rig (top right), component assembly (bottom right) and construction.

where absolutely needed, and uniquely sized where a failure in the stress-testing rig demanded a more rigid component. In total, four months were spent steaming, bending and assembling the entire lightweight roof sections within the assembly workshop at Hooke Park. Once completed, the large swatches of structure were craned into position (Figure 11.8), temporarily supported by a continuous scaffold deck and then seamed together. Nodes were then connected sequentially until the entire reciprocal grillage was completed (Figure 11.9).

Conclusion

Aᴸᴸ parties came together in an approach that translates the potentials of a context into the potentials of architecture. It was equally valuable to spend time computing, testing, working in the wood shop and forest, and discussing the project goals with the community. Beyond a

Figure 11.8

Once prefabricated in the workshop, three large swatches of structure were lifted into position atop of a tiered scaffolding deck.

Figure 11.9
All elements were finally connected onsite, in-situ, atop of a tiered scaffolding deck.

pragmatic space for the storage of wood, this simple architectural brief can be utilized as an opportunity to rethink and reinterpret contemporary ideologies. Collective goals of sustainability, efficiency, and economic viability, combined with a reappraisal of traditional techniques, and the potentials of computation produced the timber seasoning shelter. At its core, the project leverages digital processes to augment thinking and strategies of material usage. These strategies, in turn, result in the architecture, its spatiality, and embedded research.

Acknowledgements

THE timber seasoning shelter at Hooke Park is the product of four students as part of their completion of the Master of Architecture course administered by the Architectural Association School of Architecture. The students are Meghan Dorrian, Kawit Ko-udomvit, Omri Menashe and Glen Stellmacher. Support was provided in terms of academic tutelage from Charley Brentnall, Charlie Corry Wright, Stewart Dodd, and Martin Self. Workshop and site supervision was provided by Charlie Corry Wright, Edward Coe, and Jack Hawker. Engineering support was provided from ARUP by Francis Archer, Toby Clark, Andrew Lawrence, and Glen Rust. Additionally, membrane supply and support was provided from Architen Landrell by Ceri Richards, Christopher Rowell, and Lance Rowell. Material testing was also administered at Bath University with Nick Gathercole. Finally, the project would not have been possible without the help of volunteers from the AA Summer Build programme, especially Francesco Fumagalli and Mark Torrens.

References

British Standard/The European Standard (1994). *Durability of Wood and Wood-based Products: Natural Durability of Solid Wood*. Part 2.EN 350-2:1994. Europe: BSI.

Goldsworthy, A. (1987). *New Milestones Project, Entrance at the Working Woodland, Hooke Park*. For the Parnham Trust, Dorset, 1986, Letter to Common Ground. London.

Office of Industrial Technologies (2001). *Forest Products: Industry of the Future*. Pamphlet. Office of Energy Efficiency and Renewable Energy, US Department of Energy.

Peck, E. (1957). *Bending Solid Wood to Form*, Agriculture Handbook 125, U.S. Department of Agriculture, Forest Service, Washington, D.C.: U.S. Government Printing Office.

Notes

1. Steam bending colloquially refers to a process in which wood is heated and wetted through the application of hot steam. This introduction of heat and moisture facilitates the plasticization of the material. For more technical information on the manipulation of wood through steam bending, see Peck (1957).

2. Supporting data has been collected within a spreadsheet through testing by the Forest Products Research Laboratory, Princess Risborough, date unknown, and acquired by personal communication with Jeremy Ralph, the Estate and Development Manager of Hooke Park.

3. 'Although the [wood products] industry meets over half of its energy needs with biomass-derived fuel, it is still the fourth-largest user of fossil energy in the U.S. manufacturing sector' (Office of Industrial Technologies 2001).

4. The average density of Hooke Park beech was found to be 562.5 kg/m^3 after a sample size of 14 pieces were tested from six different trees from different parts of the forest using the oven dry method. The specimens were planted in 1954, making them 59 years old at the time of analysis.

12

Hooke Park Biomass Boiler House

Yingzi Wang

Architectural Association School of Architecture, England

As a result of standardization in the timber industry, only a fraction of the available raw material is deemed suitable for construction. Yingzi Wang, graduate of the Architectural Association's Design & Make MArch programme, introduces the Hooke Park Biomass Boiler House. In this full scale experimental building, a new methodology is proposed that is driven by the irregular form of natural materials. It suggests that by employing emerging 3D scanning technologies, the abundantly available irregularly shaped raw timber available in the forests can be put to use, enabling a renaissance of the use of irregularly shaped material in architecture. This research not only opens up the opportunity to make use of inherently advantageous properties of what is currently considered 'defective' timber, but also aims to find new design applications of naturally formed timber in architecture, potentially contributing to a new and expanded timber market.

Introduction

The Hooke Park Biomass Boiler House project involved testing of a 3D-scanning process of standing curved trees, as well as the application of the resulting scanning data to derive an architectural geometry. The intention of the project, which was carried out by two students of the Architectural Association's Design & Make MArch programme, was to demonstrate that trees with no value in conventional forestry terms can be intelligently applied in architecture. The new capabilities of low-cost 3D scanning, combined with digital extraction and processing of the scan data enabled an expression of naturally formed geometry in the constructed building. This approach opens new opportunities to exploit natural timber forms in architecture, and increases the economic potential of locally grown timber.

The brief for the project was to design and construct a building that would house a biomass boiler, a buffer tank and a woodchip bunker for the district heating system of the Hooke Park campus. Replacing oil boilers and electric heating, the project is part of a larger plan to establish a closed sustainable cycle for heating by using timber waste from the 150-hectare Hooke Park woodland. Low value timber from forestry thinning operations and waste from sawmilling and workshop operations will provide the fuel for the system.

The building is located centrally on the Hooke Park campus, between the existing workshop, the Prototype House, and the Westminster Lodge. It is positioned into an existing slope to simplify the delivery of woodchips through a hatch at roof level (Figure 12.1). The design intent was to read the building as a continuation of the topological contours of the site; this is expressed through layering of the building structure and a curved flow of the building walls.

The identification of an area of trees with naturally grown curvature (described by foresters as 'basal sweep') led to the idea that a variant of traditional log-cabin construction could be developed using these curved elements to generate a material-inspired free-form wall. Each tree was about 20 years old and, as a consequence of growing on a steep hillside, had developed quite extreme sweeps in the lower few metres of their trunks (Figure 12.2). Several hundreds of these trees populate the woodland, but from a forestry perspective they have no value, as they cannot be economically processed into sawn wood products or even chipped for biomass fuel. Conversely, from a designer's perspective, the natural geometry offered a compelling formal architectural potential.

The building is divided into a plant room and a chip store, and the envelope of these two rooms is made of curved and straight timber, sitting on a 150mm thick concrete retaining wall, which is mostly below ground level. The roof of the boiler house is flat and accessible, with a structure comprising of timber joists spanning across, above which a Kerto Laminated-Veneer-Lumber deck has been placed for additional support. The roof is accessible from the road level, with a curved balustrade wall following the edge, forming a flowing surface matching the timber wall below.

Figure 12.1

Concept model: layering of the building structure and flowing into Hooke Park landscape.

Figure 12.2
Naturally bent Douglas fir in the forest of Hooke Park.

3D scanning

THE first challenge for the project was to get the geometrical information of each standing bent tree. The first method tested was a photographic record from which the two-dimensional curve of a tree was extracted. However, this information was not accurate enough for further design and construction, because most trees were curving in three dimensions. Instead, a gaming system sensor was used to 3D scan the trees and efficiently collect 3D geometric data. The scanning technology is based on a time-of-flight system in which a short pulse of light is sent and the time taken for the reflected light to return is used to estimate the distance to points on the scanned surface (Bernardini & Rushmeier, 2002).

Using interface software, scanning parameters were defined, including boundary box size, scanned object type and scan quality. The boundary box was necessary in order to get rid of irrelevant surrounding data, particularly bushes and branches around the target tree. The scanning process was executed by one or two persons standing one to two meters away from the tree, rotating the scanner to capture the tree trunk, moving upwards from the roots (Figure 12.3).

Figure 12.3
Scanning trees in the forest.

The scanning positions were chosen in such a way that there was a clean view of the trunk, while avoiding overhead light coming through the tree canopy.

As the scanner is sensitive to direct sunlight, a few trees could not be scanned outdoors; these trees were moved into Hooke Park's assembly workshop and hung from the roof trusses to continue the scanning. Here, without the direct light, the scanner could operate in a range of up to seven metres. In total, 155 trees were scanned in the forest and numbered (Figure 12.4), and another 110 trees or tree segments were extracted from the forest and scanned indoors. These tests confirmed that outdoor scanning was less favourable than indoor scanning due to accessibility issues, unfavourable lighting conditions and unpredictable weather conditions.

The scanning device could be moved around, so the target tree could be scanned from multiple perspectives. Movements had to be gentle and slow in order for the computer to process and match the various views. The most efficient method was to allow the computer scripts to attach a scan to the existing calculation after each iteration. The scanning output consists of a digital triangulated mesh containing thousands of vertex points. To organize the 3D fragmented tree, a script found a series of best-fit arcs through cross-sections of the point set and then completed the circles. The resulting circles describe the changing diameter of the tree. Through the centre points of these circles, a central curve was generated, representing the curvature of each tree (Figures 12.5 and 12.6). To extract the maximum sawn diameter from each tree, the script also calculated the best position for sawing in order to use the available material as efficiently as possible. Through these physical and digital processes, a tree database was constructed containing 3D models and a spreadsheet of tapering diameter, changing curvature, best sawing position and maximum depth.

Figure 12.4
Samples of original trees and scanned meshes.

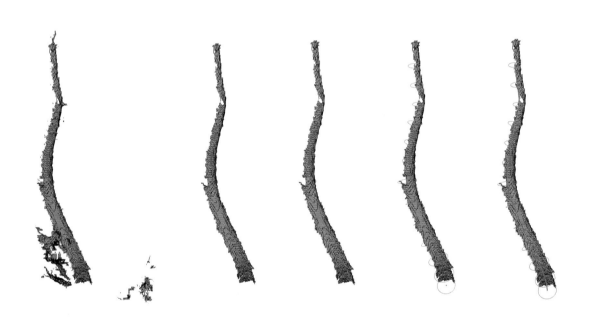

Figure 12.5
Digital processes to extract tapering diameter and central curve of the tree.

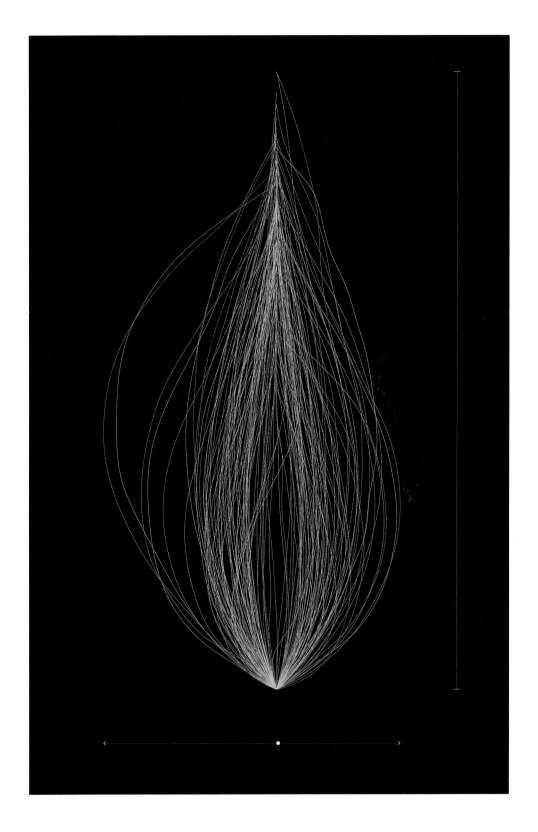

Figure 12.6
Central curve range of the tree.

Geometry definition

I**N** parallel with collating the database of the tree geometries, techniques were developed for determining the arrangement of the tree components within the building's wall. Digital script routines were written to automate the process of iteratively test-fitting all the tree curves and optimizing the wall geometry with respect to different criteria. This approach meant that the computer could rapidly test and refine many variations for the wall, and could continue to adapt the wall shape in response to the realities found during the fabrication of the actual timber components. Several strategies were developed to define the geometry of the stacked wall. One approach started with an ideal given wall surface from which a set of horizontal target curves was extracted. The script then tested all available tree components at a sequence of positions along each target curve, finding the one with the smallest distance between the tree curve and the target curve. Once established, the best-fit log was kept in position and removed from the available set of components (Figure 12.7). The second approach optimized the tree segment placement for tangent continuity. By setting the tangency of tree segment ends as the criteria to look for the next tree component to join, thousands of smooth and continuous curves were generated.

The limitation of the first (best-fit) strategy was that it could not always find a well-fitting tree segment due to the curvature differences between the given form and the available pieces. Conversely, the latter strategy (tangential joint) was able to generate thousands of interesting combinations of separated curves, but these curves did not form a continuous surface. Therefore a third strategy was developed that considered both goals in an iterative process. Some key courses from the original tree curves identified the unique geometry, and then the matching process started again to find the other suitable tree segments. This way, a more natural, smoothly flowing progression of geometry was generated. The key courses were allowed to overlap, thus creating vertically connected points, which contributed to the wall's structural stability. While controlling natural variation through a digital process, this strategy successfully shows the character of the raw timber itself.

The large range in diameter of timber was a factor that affected the final design. Traditionally, carpenters select trees with minimal tapering for log-cabin construction (Chambers, 2003). Digital scanning and use of scripts enabled strongly tapered trees to be used with minimal waste, by grouping trees with similar diameters. For each course, the script would only use trees from a single group within a certain diameter range. As a result, the height of the courses varies and the amount of waste is limited. For structural considerations, the group with the largest diameter is used for the bottom course; as the wall becomes higher, the course height decreases. Overall, 20 courses were generated from five thickness groups.

Figure 12.7 (facing page)

Digital arrangements of the tree through best-fit strategy.

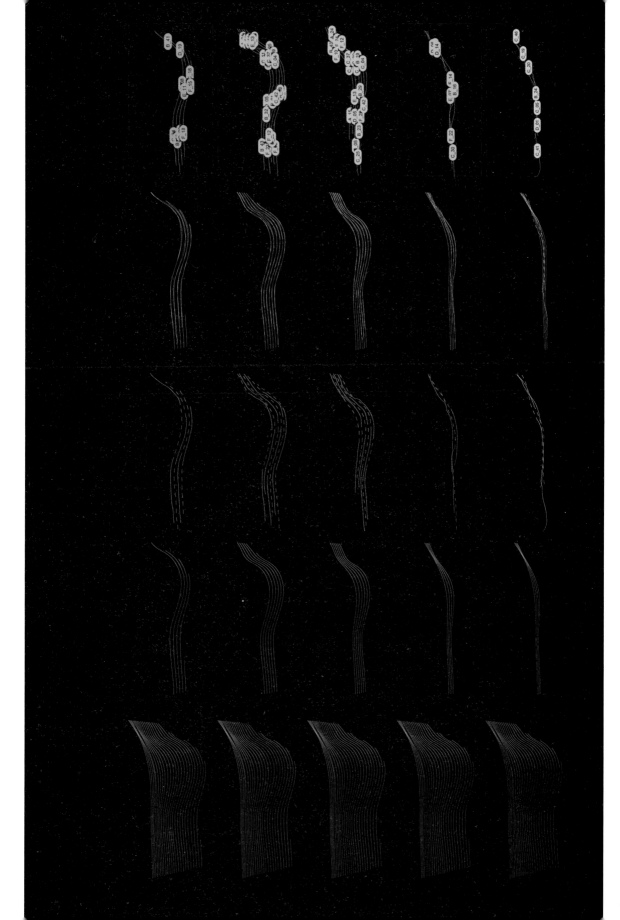

Fabrication and details

To achieve a durable log wall made of unseasoned wood, particular details were incorporated in the fabrication and connection of the logs. There were five processes involved in the prefabrication process, including milling, chamfer cutting, drip cutting, relief grooving, and de-barking. In the sawing process, a mobile, modified band saw/chainsaw was designed to allow free movement to saw the top and bottom of the curving logs (Figure 12.8). By pivoting the chainsaw, an angle cut was applied to each log, thus forming a chamfer for rain water dispersal. A 6mm wide drip cut was created, which was always above the chamfer edge of the lower course to keep water away. Additionally, a relief cut was designed to pre-release the pressure that results from the shrinking and seasoning of the wood. This helped to avoid future timber splitting in other places. De-barking was required to prevent the bark of the tree catching water and nursing microorganisms that rot logs. All of these processes aimed to expand the durability of timber without any chemical treatment.

Between the courses of the log wall, a 15mm air gap was incorporated, which helped keeping the timber dry and useable for processing. Oak packers placed every 600mm along the curves formed the connections between courses, and wood wedges were used where large deviations between courses occurred. In order to tie the courses, wood screws were applied through all the packers and wedges. These details are based on the material properties and evolved from traditional methods of wood construction. Fabrication and construction were carried out with the help of 20 summer volunteers guided by local carpenters.

Figure 12.8
Modified chainsaw allowing free movement to saw the top, bottom and chamfer cuts of the bent logs.

Natural form timber

HISTORICALLY, the Primitive Hut (Rykwert, 1981), the Tudor ship building (Matthew, 1831), and the Medieval Cruck Timber-Framing (Charles, 1967) each provide vivid examples that demonstrate the possibilities of using timber in its various natural forms. While trees grow, each fibre in the material contributes to the tree's overall structure and form. This fact was well understood by traditional ship builders, who knew that making a straight object out of a curved piece of timber reduces its strength, and, conversely, making a curved object out of a straight piece of timber does the same. The Biomass Boiler House shows an alternative and more efficient way to make use of naturally growing forms, rather than reshaping them with expensive and energy intensive technology. Today's timber market restricts itself to a single standard, thus missing the opportunity to use wood to its full technical and architectural potential.

Today's advanced and easily accessible 3D scanning technology can open up new applications of naturally shaped timber in architecture. In the UK, this technology has already been successfully applied to scan parcels of forest, for example in Kielder Water and Forest Park by ScanLAB (Sheil, 2014), and a forest in East Sussex by Universal Assembly Unit.[1] At Hooke Park, this application has been pushed further by utilizing scanning data for design and full-scale construction. This scanned and digitally recorded tree data inspires and assists architectural design intelligently, and contributes to efficient timber construction methods. It opens a new understanding of useful timber: a natural resource with diverse form, no longer limited to standardized products from regularized, straight trees (Figures 12.9 and 12.10).

The rethought and rejuvenation of naturally formed timber can potentially give rise to a new timber market. Furthermore, the integration of this new digital approach provokes more creative architectural design and construction based on these locally and naturally grown timber elements.

Acknowledgements

THE Biomass Boiler House is a project of Design & Make MArch Students Sattaveesa Sahu and Yingzi Wang of Architectural Association's School of Architecture. It would not have been possible without the academic instruction from Martin Self, Kate Darby, Charley Brentnall, Charlie Corry Wright, and Jason Griffiths, and the technical support from Jeremy Ralph, Oscar Emanuel, James Stubbs, Edward Coe, Jack Hawker, Christopher Sadd, James Vooght and Merry Hinsley. Engineering support was provided from ARUP by Charlotte Briggs and Coco Van Egeraat. Also importantly, it was accomplished with the help of 20 excellent summer builders.

Figure 12.10
Finished building sitting in the landscape.

Figure 12.9 (facing page)
Finished building.

References

Bernardini, F. & Rushmeier, H. (2002). The 3D Model Acquisition Pipeline. *Computer Graphics Forum*, 21(2), 149–172.

Chambers, R.W. (2003). *Log Construction Manual: The Ultimate Guide to Building Handcrafted Log Homes*. River Falls, WI: Deep Stream Press.

Charles, F.W.B. (1967). *Medieval Cruck: Building and its Derivatives*. The Society for Medieval Archaeology.

Matthew, P. (1831). *On Naval Timber and Arboriculture*. Neil & Co. Printers.

Rykwert, J. (1981). *On Adam's House in Paradise: The Idea of the Primitive Hut in Architectural History* (2nd edn). Cambridge, MA: MIT Press.

Sheil, B. (2014). *Architectural Design*, 84(1), special issue, *High Definition: Zero Tolerance in Design and Production AD*. Hoboken: Wiley.

Note

1. Universal Assembly Unit (2014), "Datum Explorer", Available at http://datumexplorer.universalassemblyunit.com/ (Accessed 4 December 2014).

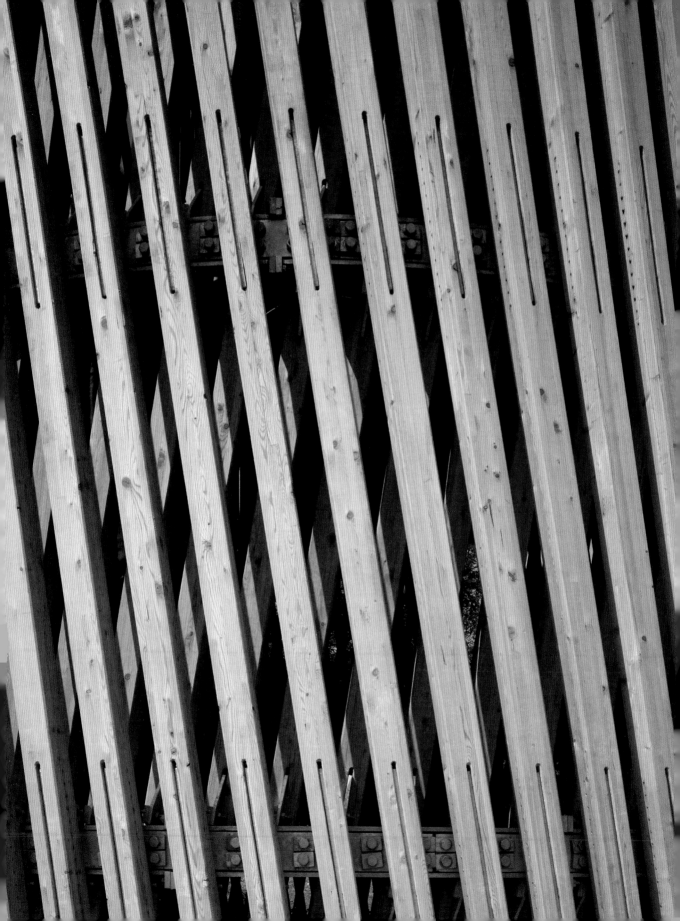

PART FIVE

Perspectives

13

Manufacturing perspectives

Tobias Schwinn[1] in conversation with
Holzbau Amann and Müllerblaustein
[1]Institute for Computational Design, University of Stuttgart, Germany

THE ability of the timber construction industry to continuously embrace technological change is remarkable given that wood, with its long history of tools and techniques, and cultural traditions, is still commonly considered a low-tech and conservative building material. However, far from being slow in adopting change or resisting innovation, an ever-growing number of innovative constructions made from wood eloquently prove the opposite. The unique interplay of technology, economic opportunity and manufacturing expertise that is at the heart of innovation in the timber construction field is the topic of conversation with two of its key representatives: Holzbau Amann GmbH and Müllerblaustein Holzbau GmbH. Using built projects as examples, Reinhold Müller and Benjamin Eisele of Müllerblaustein and Fredy Oberle and Wolfgang Müll of Holzbau Amann offer their individual perspectives regarding the impact of technology on business, timber construction and collaboration. The conversation about the current state of the digitalisation of design and manufacturing is framed on the one hand by a retrospection of the technology-driven changes in building practice within the last 20 years, and on the other by a speculation about possible future developments in the field.

The digital turn in timber manufacturing

STARTING in the 1980s and accelerating in the 1990s, a first wave of automation and computerisation of fabrication unfolded within the manufacturing industry with the advent of computer numerically controlled (CNC) machinery. In the case of timber construction, existing methods of manual joinery on-site and on the shop floor started being replaced by automated joinery machines. While this first generation of CNC-machines mainly aimed at automating existing fabrication techniques, they imposed specific limits on control and kinematic capabilities, based on their early software and hardware, thereby defining the economics, the range of producible geometry, and the applicability of the machines.

First steps towards computer aided manufacturing

THE timber construction companies Amann, founded in 1932, and Müllerblaustein, founded in 1945, are both exemplary for the deep social and cultural roots of timber construction in Central Europe. At the same time, their company history also illustrates the technological development that unfolded particularly since the 1980s.

Both companies invested in automated joinery machines in the early 1990s and were considered early adopters. The introduction of CNC-machinery, however, was preceded in the 1970s and 1980s by the use of mathematical methods in carpentry where the dimensions and locations of cuts were calculated using trigonometry and traced on the stock pieces on the shop floor to facilitate prefabrication. According to Benjamin Eisele this approach was 'a precondition and a first step towards digitalisation and the adoption of automated joinery'. A specific large-scale project, the new campus for the University of Ulm, a contract, which Müllerblaustein won in 1989, then triggered the adoption of automated joinery: the delivery of the required volume of timber within the given time frame and budget was only economically viable through the automation of joinery.

Initial hurdles of digitalisation

EVEN though automated joinery had soon proven its usefulness, it was seen critically by the community, Reinhold Müller remembers. First, machining identical beams sequentially was slower than the manual process where multiple beams could be cut at once; second, the quality of the automated cuts was initially inferior to the manual ones; and third, in engineered timber structures the metal connectors had to be inserted manually and, consequently, the automation was not complete. The additional planning and handling effort required by automated joinery therefore had to be justified by either the complexity or the volume of fabrication – a criticism that is still valid today.

With the introduction first of calculated joinery and later automated joinery, timber construction essentially changed from a manual craft to an industrial production process: in the beginning, even just 30 years ago, there was still time to manually chisel out a timber joint, but with the increasing pace of the construction industry, manually produced joints, such as mortise and tenon joints, became unfeasible. Therefore integrated joints were increasingly replaced by joints that could be produced more economically and by using metal plate connectors – in the words of Fredy Oberle 'a disaster for carpentry'. This development, however, was not only due to automation but also due to a structural approach for calculating timber joints, which could not adequately account for the reduced cross-sections of beams at the joint locations.

In order to control its new machinery, the timber construction industry adopted software from other industries, primarily automotive and metal forming, however not without its own specific limitations. The economics of fabrication and especially milling in those industries is decidedly different from timber construction: there three-dimensional moulds can be milled in a time-intensive three-axis configuration using a ball mill assuming that the mould is later used to churn out many identical parts; whereas in timber construction each piece is produced individually and sequentially, even if geometrically identical, which requires a more time-effective fabrication approach. Consequently, timber fabricators often had to improvise in order to achieve the necessary efficiency, Oberle explains. Interestingly, the machine hardware has hardly changed over time, but the control software has evolved a lot and it is only now possible to take full advantage of the kinematic potential of the machines.

Despite initial scepticism, automated joinery and the associated digital planning process is now state-of-the-art and firms like Amann and Müllerblaustein have proven its usefulness and competitive advantage in many projects covering a wide spectrum of timber construction ranging from institutional projects such as the Centre Pompidou in Metz or the National Park Centre in Garmisch, to engineered timber structures such as the Messe Friedrichshafen or the Jüberg Tower in Hemer, to boutique projects such as the Hermès Rive Gauche in Paris or the Landesgartenschau Exhibition Hall in Schwäbisch Gmünd (see Chapter 8), to finally the large field of residential construction.

Consequences of digitalisation in timber manufacturing

As it is the case in many other industries, increasing digitalisation and automation also had significant effects not only on the economics and established techniques of timber construction, but also on the collaboration among the different disciplines within the field. Progress in digital fabrication, regarding machine design and control, combined with more timber-specific structural calculation methods now allows for the efficient realisation of integral and even geometrically complex joints such as dovetail joints, within the economic constraints of the contemporary building industry. This is considered a huge innovation as traditional and highly differentiated joint types offer new possibilities for contemporary timber construction that were out of reach only 15 years ago, and which, Reinhold Müller adds, also reduce the amount of additional fasteners and steel in the timber joints. Another obvious benefit of digital fabrication, according to Wolfgang Müll, is the much higher accuracy of fabrication, which results in reduced construction times on site.

Non-standard construction

Whereas the first wave of digitalisation was geared towards the automation of existing techniques within the serial production paradigm, the field is currently experiencing a second wave of digital fabrication facilitated by the widespread use of parametric design methods and aimed at achieving geometric variability of building components, while keeping the economic benefits of automation. Müller states that timber construction today, even in conventional projects, is essentially following the one-off production paradigm. This development, combined with technical skills and the carpenter's innate motivation to do the exceptional, provides a fertile ground on which advances in wood architecture can occur. Asked about this particular motivation, Müll speculates that it might have to do with the fact that 'the carpenter has always had the experience of being exposed on top of a structure and naturally wants to stand out'. While, from his point of view, the overall amount of non-standard work is certainly increasing, the number of timber construction companies that operate in this segment of the market is also growing. A new generation of consulting firms that specialise in information modelling, complex geometry, the interface between computer aided design (CAD) and computer aided manufacturing (CAM), and even machine control, naturally offer their services to many possible clients. Such collaborations have made projects like the Centre Pompidou-Metz viable and are now becoming more common-place.

Centre Pompidou-Metz, France, 2010

Architecture: Shigeru Ban and Jean de Gastines, Tokyo, Paris
Timber construction: Holzbau Amann GmbH, Weilheim-Bannholz
Structural design: Ove Arup, London; Hermann Blumer, Waldstatt

The curved timber grid shell of the Centre Pompidou-Metz (Figure 13.1) with its characteristic tri-hexagonal pattern and translucent fibreglass-reinforced membrane unites under one roof exhibition and event spaces, restaurant areas, and a spacious entrance hall. A hexagon in plan, the timber structure is suspended from a 77m tall central mast and transforms into four funnel-shaped columns in four of the six corners. The result is a geometrically complex free-form surface with a surface area of 8,500m² and spans of up to 40m that is materialised using prefabricated double-curved timber beams (Figures 13.2 and 13.3). These beams have been custom glue-laminated and CNC-milled to meet their individual target geometry. A main constraint of the subtractive milling process was to maintain the fibre continuity of the wood lamellas in the beam by limiting all cuts to less than five degrees relative to the fibre direction.

Figure 13.1

Night-time view of the Centre Pompidou-Metz showing the characteristic translucent roof structure.

© Roland Halbe

Figure 13.2

A close-up view of the double-curved timber beams during prefabrication.

© Holzbau Amann

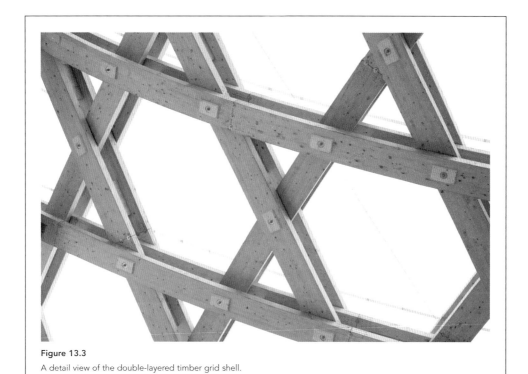

Figure 13.3

A detail view of the double-layered timber grid shell.

© *designtoproduction*

Advances in prefabrication

BOTH companies evidently aim for a high level of prefabrication in their work. While Benjamin Eisele points out that prefabrication is the pre-condition for meeting completion dates and quality expectations, Reinhold Müller even goes so far as to say that prefabrication permeates every consideration of the firm: from project selection, pricing, structural design, and detail design, all the way to the worker on site who assembles the building components.

The topic of prefabrication in timber construction, however, is still evolving as Wolfgang Müll observes. From the point of view of Amann, it does not make sense, economically as well as ecologically, to haul huge glulam or cross-laminated timber-elements through the countryside from the manufacturer to the timber fabricator and then on to the construction site. Especially, since manufacturers of laminated timber products have themselves started to invest in automated joinery and are now able to ship building elements that can go from the saw mill straight to the site based on the specifications of a carpenter. As a consequence, some fabricators have effectively outsourced joinery altogether and focus instead on the on-site assembly of pre-formatted elements. This development begs the question whether there might be a tendency that timber fabricators won't invest in automated joinery anymore if it can be so easily outsourced. While this might be an option for smaller firms, Müll says, Amann is aiming for maximising the amount of work that they can do in-house because this is where they can add value. And this strategy works particularly well with geometrically complex building elements, because timber manufacturers and joinery centres rely on simple geometries and serial production to achieve volume and competitive prices.

Current limitations

WHEN it comes to the limitations of the current digital design and fabrication process in timber construction, which is subsumed in the term Digital Chain, several topics come up repeatedly during the conversations: first, the limitations of the subtractive fabrication process itself, such as milling and sawing, as it applies to the anisotropic material wood; second the multiplicity of applicable norms and regional building codes in Germany that are inhibiting and stifling innovation; and finally the topic of data exchange, design changes and the still limited ability to accommodate those changes efficiently.

The first limitation becomes apparent in the production of curved and particularly double-curved timber components, where the challenge is to maintain fibre continuity so as to maintain the load-bearing capacity of the wood. According to Wolfgang Müll, the glulam industry has not really evolved in the direction of double-curved elements, and their fabrication continues to be very inefficient and therefore costly. Geometrically unique single-curved elements are already problematic because of the time it takes to laminate each piece: even when using an automated clamping system, every beam blocks the mould for at least seven hours. In the case of double-curved beams, the effort becomes excessive, either from a manual labour point of view when a three-dimensional curve is constructed out of a myriad of individual lamellas; or from a material waste point of view when an initially single-curved beam is milled down to achieve double-curvature, which not only disrupts the wood fibres but also generates a lot of waste. According to Müll, the solution would be an automated glue-lamination machine that can bend the timber lamellas based on a three-dimensional blueprint, but, 'realistically', he adds, 'the market might just be too small for any machine manufacturer to invest in its engineering'.

The other major limiting factor is the data translation process between architectural design, structural engineering and timber construction, which is still slow and tedious. The process of modelling fabrication information in CAM software packages and its transfer onto the machine is defined by a lot of re-modelling and additional work that does not accommodate design changes very well. To make this effort worthwhile, the milling geometry has to either be part of a digital catalogue, and a lot of volume can be produced, or sufficiently complex. In any case, optimising the fabrication data generation would help a lot, Reinhold Müller remarks. From this point of view, he continues, the Landesgartenschau Exhibition Hall (see Chapter 8) constitutes a huge leap in timber construction: controlling the machinery from within the design environment, saves a lot of time, effort, and money.

Digital collaboration

Regarding the collaboration between architects, engineers and timber fabricators, Benjamin Eisele notes that the level of integration between disciplines has noticeably increased in the last decade. Whereas in the past, an architect often presented a completed design to the fabricator, nowadays the conversation starts a lot earlier. Not only has the frequency of data exchange increased between architects, engineers and fabricators, but at the same time the amount of information per exchange has decreased, which allows for a higher level of integration. On the other hand, the validity of digital information is also decreasing because it can be so easily changed, which makes the issue of design changes more relevant. Parametric and associative design methods obviously make things a lot easier than they used to be, even ten years ago, but still there is no optimal way of dealing with design changes. Rather than trying to avoid design changes, Wolfgang Müll proposes that they should be embraced as a challenge and as a natural part of an integrative design process.

According to Reinhold Müller, the integrative nature of timber construction, which not only covers structural aspects, but also thermal requirements of the building envelope, and even acoustic and aesthetic requirements of interior design, mandates a holistic digital planning approach. An example of such an integrative planning process is the Jüberg-Turm project, where 'digitalisation had to be maximised or else the project would never have worked out'. (See Chapter 14.)

Another significant development in the industry that Müller has observed is a growing sense in the field that all the stakeholders of the design process are 'in the same boat' and that there is an increasing awareness of the interconnectedness between design, engineering and fabrication. A consequence of this development is that architectural design is becoming more timber-specific – an observation that is seconded by Müll, who adds that some architects, for example Barkow Leibinger, even ask about fabrication possibilities during the concept design stage. Specifically in the Trumpf cafeteria project, Amann was able to deliver input at a very early design stage, which from a carpenter's point of view is very satisfying: 'the earlier the better', Müll says. Besides his personal interest, being part of the design development or even concept design stage on the architect's side would be beneficial for everyone because of higher quality and reduced costs – except that clients usually are afraid of committing to a contractor early on because they think they won't get the best price. As a consequence many decisions are effectively postponed until after tender stage, when finally a contractor is on-board, but where making changes becomes really costly.

Trumpf Campus Restaurant, Ditzingen, Germany, 2008

Architecture: Barkow Leibinger, Berlin
Timber construction: Holzbau Amann GmbH, Weilheim-Bannholz
Structural design: Werner Sobek Stuttgart

The Trumpf Campus Restaurant provides a central cafeteria and event space for the company's industrial campus and headquarters (Figures 13.4 and 13.5). Its characteristic roof is a wide-spanning polygonal canopy resting on seven column-pairs. The main load-bearing structure consists of steel trusses that span between the columns and the polygonal glue-laminated timber cells that fill the area between the trusses. The polygonal cells are geometrically as well as functionally differentiated and function either as skylights with solar-glass (Figure 13.6), as perforated wood acoustic panels, or as artificial lighting cells. A critical aspect was the economical prefabrication of all geometrically unique timber elements and their close to 300 individual joints, which was only possible using computer-controlled fabrication processes.

Figure 13.4
View of the Trumpf Campus Restaurant under construction.
© David Franck

Figure 13.5
The finished main interior space.
© David Franck

Figure 13.6
A detail view of the polygonal timber-framed skylights.
© David Franck

Future developments

New approaches

HYBRID construction approaches are perceived as a growing trend that has the potential to expand the share of timber construction into areas that are currently dominated by steel and concrete. Reinhold Müller offers a number of examples for hybrid constructions with growth potential including building envelopes and unitised systems made from wood; but also hybrid concrete and timber slabs systems, which offer the advantage of functional integration over established systems. In these applications, timber not only constitutes a lost formwork, but also the tension zone in the slab, which can enable extremely slender profiles with very large spans. Additionally, these slabs can even include a finished ceiling surface with integrated acoustical properties. Both possibilities are demonstrated by the National Park Centre 'Haus der Berge' in Berchtesgaden, Germany. Furthermore, given that the share of timber construction in single-family housing in the state of Baden-Württemberg grew from 5% to 25% within a few years, hybrid approaches have the potential to further increase the share of timber particularly in multi-storey residential construction. And finally, hybrid approaches are also expected to increase their share in civil engineering structures, such as heavy-load timber bridges, where the timber again acts as the tension zone and constitutes a lost formwork for the concrete.

National Park Centre 'Haus der Berge', Berchtesgaden, Germany, 2013

Architecture: Staatliches Bauamt Traunstein with Leitenbacher Spiegelberger Architekten BDA, Traunstein
Timber construction: Müllerblaustein Holzbau GmbH, Blaustein
Structural design: Seeberger, Friedl & Partner, Munich

The National Park Visitor Centre 'Haus der Berge' functions as educational centre and showcase for the ecology and protection of the alpine environment (Figures 13.7 and 13.8). The project stands out for its innovation in the development of a high-performing hybrid concrete-timber slab system that is characterised by spans of up-to 16m, high acoustical requirements, and by particularly slender slab thicknesses (Figure 13.9). High-performing engineered timber boards in conjunction with cambered glulam-beams act as lost formwork for the concrete layer. With the concrete mainly acting in compression and the timber in tension, the shear forces at their interface are accommodated through the same screws that connect timber boards and beams as well as through adding grooves into the timber boards that run perpendicular to the span.

Figure 13.7

View of the main entrance of the completed National Park Centre.

© Josephine Unterhauser

Figure 13.8

Under construction.

© Müllerblaustein

Figure 13.9

A view of the concrete-timber hybrid slab before the pouring of the concrete.

© Staatliches Bauamt Traunstein

Other approaches that specifically take advantage of the inherent physical properties of wood are also expected to become more commonplace. An example is the Hermès Rive Gauche project where the elasticity of wood is used strategically during fabrication (See Chapter 14). The challenge of course with elastic bending is to accurately account for the spring back of the wood, where the desired shapes of the elements are different from the ones that have to be produced. While this project is part of the furniture or interior design domain rather than the established timber construction domain, Wolfgang Müll estimates that it is a market that timber construction can serve particularly well, because 'it is hard to imagine it being done in steel'.

In the Hermès project, the elasticity of the wood was used as the defining property during fabrication, which begs the question whether there are examples for the active use of elasticity in structural applications. Müll responds that while in theory active bending is a brilliant approach, because the final form emerges as part of the tensioning process, the fact that this approach has not been developed further since Julius Natterer and Frei Otto used it in 1972 for the Olympic Ice Skating Rink in Munich and 1975 for the Multihalle in Mannheim hints at some inherent problems. Most importantly, the creeping of the wood, which effectively reduces the tension in the material and consequently changes its structural state, is hard to incorporate into the planning process. A project, however, where Amann did use the bending elasticity of wood for structural advantage is the Zollinger roof of the Messe Friedrichshafen, Germany, made in collaboration with Merz, Kaufmann & Partner in 2002.

Messe Friedrichshafen, Germany, 2002

Architecture: gmp von Gerkan, Marg & Partners, Hamburg
Timber construction: Holzbau Amann GmbH, Weilheim-Bannholz
Structural design: Merz & Kaufmann, Dornbirn

The hall (Figure 13.10) is part of a group of eight halls on the Lake Constance New Trade Fair grounds and is covered by a timber roof spanning 68 by 150 metres and column-free, providing ample exhibition space. The roof is a Zollinger system (Figure 13.11) composed of individual short beams arranged in a diamond-shaped grid with a sub-span made of steel rods (Figure 13.12). This sub-span is post-tensioned not only to cancel out the lateral forces at the support points but also 'heightened' in order to avoid any compression members in the diagonals of the truss. The tension in each diagonal therefore had to be carefully tuned with regards to the self-weight of the roof in order to avoid any displacement at the support points – a strategy, which is only possible due to the elasticity of the timber. On site this was implemented by manually calibrating a turnbuckle screw in each diagonal to achieve the right tension.

Figure 13.10
View of the exterior of the hall showing the Zollinger system.
© Jürgen Schmidt

Figure 13.11
View of the interior of the hall showing the Zollinger system.
© Jürgen Schmidt

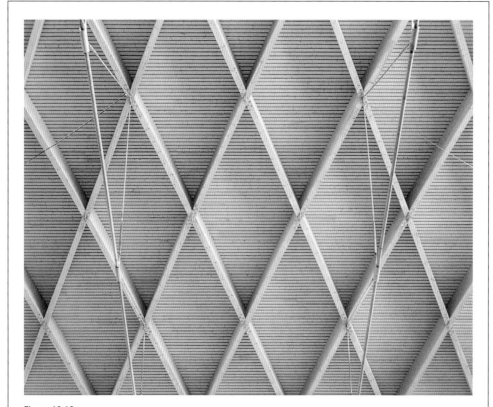

Figure 13.12
Close-up view of the timber dia-grid including the horizontal sub-span.
© Jürgen Schmidt

The roof, which spans 60 metres, column-free, uses a diagonally braced sub-span that is post-tensioned in such a way as to cancel out the self-weight of the roof in order to avoid any compression members in the diagonals of the truss. These kinds of complex projects that require innovative structural solutions effectively demonstrate that successful timber construction really depends on the quality of timber-specific structural engineering, Müll emphasises. But also from the point of view of digital fabrication, this project is illustrative: while there is significant repetition in the timber elements of the vault-shaped Zollinger system, each of its structural members is slightly twisted allowing all the steel connectors to be made identical. 'It is a lot easier to differentiate the timber elements than it is to differentiate the steel elements', Müll explains.

Future visions

Reinhold Müller and Benjamin Eisele share the enthusiasm for naturally curved timber that drives Hooke Park's experiments (see Chapters 10–12) and the related architectural possibilities. They can imagine a future in timber construction where structural systems can be developed in response to the anatomy of trees: 'imagine a timber version of the tree columns of the Stuttgart airport', Eisele speculates. This vision where drones create vast databases of tree shapes would allow the twenty-first-century implementation of a traditional building method: one, which was once practiced in ship building and church building in the pre-industrial era prior to the advent of steel, concrete, and engineered timber products. At the same time this development could address the challenge in the production of double-curved glulam beams.

Another area where Müller expects significant progress is in the domain of man–machine collaboration. Especially tasks that are either logistically complex or dangerous and detrimental to health, such as applying coatings or lifting heavy components, could be done better in collaboration with robots. With regards to further automation, he stresses that flexibility is as critical as depth: on the one hand, a robot should be able to be used not only for process-specific automation such as milling and sawing, but also for gluing, palletising or handling, and positioning of elements; on the other hand, automation should not only address the timber, but also integrate building systems, electricity, plumbing, façade, shading, etc. all the while maintaining geometric flexibility.

Finally, Reinhold Müller imagines a future where architects, programmers, structural engineers, carpenters, electrical and HVAC (heating, ventilating and air conditioning) engineers work collaboratively around a shared and unified data model from which the fabrication machinery can be controlled directly; a future where robots intelligently interact with workers on the construction site. 'The idea', he says, 'is 20 years old, but only now we are slowly getting there'.

The enthusiasm for advancing their profession that the author experienced in the conversations with Holzbau Amann and Müllerblaustein led the field of timber construction to absorb technological change in the past and, consequently, made it an adequate reflection of the state of contemporaneous construction technology. This same enthusiasm will mean that future technological innovations in the fields of manufacturing, robotics, and information technology, and particularly their on-going confluence, will be eagerly adopted in timber construction. Finally, it is up to architects to take advantage of and to adequately account for the emerging possibilities in the architectural design process.

Acknowledgements

This article is the result of two extended conversations with Müllerblaustein Holzbau on 12 August 2015 in Blaustein and with Holzbau Amann on 2 February 2015 in Weilheim. Some statements may have been modified and condensed for clarity. The author would like to thank both firms for their candidness and for the considerable amount of time they dedicated to the conversations.

14

Engineering perspectives

Oliver David Krieg[1] in conversation with
Manfred Grohmann and Jan Knippers
[1]Institute for Computational Design, University of Stuttgart, Germany

THE advance of computational design, simulation and fabrication has significantly expanded the possibilities of timber structures and related engineering approaches in recent years. Standard timber products and conventional construction systems are rethought and hybridised, leading to more complex, efficient and innovative structures. Integrative design methods enable architects and engineers to collaborate on projects from an early design stage on, enabling the synthesis of material characteristics, structural performance, and manufacturing. Computational tools allow engineers to better integrate and utilise wood's specific anisotropic and hetero-geneous material properties, and they also enable easier communication and exchange of know-how between architects, engineers, and manufacturers, ultimately increasing the potential for innovation on all sides. Along a number of projects of their respective offices, the two interna-tionally renowned structural engineers Manfred Grohmann, co-founder of Bollinger + Grohmann Ingenieure, and Jan Knippers, co-founder of Knippers Helbig Advanced Engineering, discuss how technological innovation influenced wood architecture in the past, which challenges it is currently facing, and where future potentials lie.

Wood construction: material-specific engineering

ENGINEERS have always considered wood to be one of the most complex building materials. Its heterogeneous structural properties and responsiveness to fluctuating environmental conditions, such as relative humidity and temperature, have made it difficult to precisely calculate. But instead of working against the behaviour, wood related trades in the preindustrial era, including ship building, furniture making and architecture, employed its material properties to their advantage. Through slow but precise manual labour, every structural element and each joint was tailored to its specific function and its location within a structure, while also wasting as little material as possible. The potentials of applying material characteristics in this way, however, has become increasingly challenging during the shift from craft-based to industrial fabrication of building elements. Faster, simpler and standardised production processes that were introduced to other sectors of the building industry in the late nineteenth century made it difficult for wood to compete. While standardised building systems were developed in conjunction with new production techniques for building materials like steel and concrete, the complexity in timber processing, where both subtractive and additive fabrication methods are necessary, made it more challenging to achieve a high degree of automation. The consequences are still noticeable today. 'Material and labour costs have changed dramatically in the last decades. Compared to labour costs, material is basically free nowadays', explains Grohmann.

However, since the end of the last century wood construction has experienced what might be called a Renaissance. Grohmann and Knippers can identify two main reasons for the rise of modern wood architecture over the last 20 years. First, the invention of computer numerical control (CNC) triggered the development of wood processing machines that digitalised subtractive fabrication methods in the 1980s. They enabled the fabrication of complex wood joints, but they also opened up the possibility of combining wood with steel connectors, thus shifting the complexity towards a building material that already had economical solutions for non-standard parts. Secondly, timber manufacturers developed a range of new building products that expanded the use of wood from beam towards plate construction systems. These material-based innovations enabled wood to leave the realm of linear components and advance to surface elements; cross laminated timber (CLT), laminated veneer lumber (LVL), as well as new hardwood plywood products can be used in a variety of shapes. But they also drove timber construction towards homogenising the material and simplifying its use. 'New timber products aim at bypassing the specific material characteristics so as to make the material more predictable. There are almost no examples in architecture that make use of wood's characteristics in the way the furniture industry has done for hundreds of years', explains Jan Knippers.

Innovations in both fabrication and material technology made it easier to work with wood and to reduce labour costs, but they did not encourage the use of the material according to its characteristics as a naturally grown tissue. Calculating the heterogeneous material in relation to climatic conditions, and considering geometric changes over time through shrinkage or creep is still a difficult undertaking: 'Using wood for geometrically complex and high performance constructions is therefore a very challenging task', Jan Knippers adds.

Both of the engineering companies have realised projects that employ the material's inherent properties to achieve higher structural stability and geometric complexity. In the Peek & Cloppenburg project from Knippers Helbig Advanced Engineering (2005), the wood's high elasticity was employed to prefabricate single-curved glulam lamellas that would later be combined into a multi-layered vertical beam. Together with additional horizontal and diagonal elements this innovative construction system acts as a shell structure almost completely independent from the concrete core.

Peek & Cloppenburg, Cologne, Germany, 2005

Architecture: Renzo Piano Building Workshop Paris
Engineering: Knippers Helbig Advanced Engineering

The new five-storey shopping mall by Peek & Cloppenburg was designed as a dome structure covered by 6,800 glass panels (Figures 14.1–14.3). The vertical glulam lamellas were prefabricated to match their required single-curved geometry. Multiple thin lamellas connect through steel profiles in order to act as one structural entity. Depending on the external loads, the number of lamellas differs from top to bottom. The overall construction allows the concrete slabs to be almost completely uncoupled from the façade.

Figure 14.1–14.3
The Peek & Cloppenburg building during manufacturing and after finished construction.

The Hermès Rive Gauche (2010) project by Bollinger Grohmann Engineers similarly uses bent-laminated wooden elements for differentiated curvatures. Three nine-millimetre strips were laminated in prefabrication to act as one stable entity, and were later connected into a grid shell on site. Both projects exemplify how a synthesis of structural performance and architectural design becomes possible through the cooperation between structural engineers and architects from an early design stage on. Grohmann explains that this close collaboration is essential for such projects: 'The fundamental difference in the Hermes project is that we worked together with the architects from the very beginning. In order to develop a design proposal that makes sense from both a structural and manufacturing point of view, every decision was discussed in an interdisciplinary team'. There are, however, few examples where the material characteristics really act as the driving force behind the design process. Although timber construction offers a large potential in conjunction with new digital design and fabrication technology, it is challenging to convey that inventive spirit into larger-scale projects. Here, questions about structural systems and design workflow become critically relevant.

Rethinking structural typologies

In order to explain how structural typologies have changed in the last decades, Manfred Grohmann begins at the nineteenth century: 'Everything that we consider a typology nowadays is basically a result of the framework theory of Karl Culmann'. Before Culmann's publication of the *Graphic Statics* in 1865 carpenters built statically highly indetermined hybrid constructions that resulted in structures with high levels of redundancy. 'But in the 50s and 60s carpenters started to work based on engineers' instructions, which basically only consisted of either a purlin roof, a couple roof, or a collar-beam roof', he adds. In the last decade, however, Grohmann and Knippers witnessed again more hybrid constructions that could not be defined by those typologies. Owing to new computational design strategies, hybrid structural systems can now be calculated relatively fast, resulting in a higher level of efficiency and adaptability.

Transcending conventional typologies has led to complex and free-form building structures that push the boundaries of fabrication technology. But the development of new building products also led to the formation of a potentially much larger market share: at present, innovation in timber construction is mostly linked to urban multi-story office and residential buildings. By overcoming the challenging requirements regarding fire safety, insulation, and structural rigidity, new digital fabrication techniques could be applicable to a much larger range of projects. 'If wood structures manage to fulfil the required regulations, they will have high potential for urban developments, refurbishments, and re-densifications', says Grohmann. However, especially for the relatively new typology of timber plate construction, geometric differentiation still seems to be a major challenge for manufacturers. Instead, the building industry is more focused on the innovation of building products that are still based on standardised and inflexible production techniques. For example, technical innovation in the last years helped prefabricated timber-concrete composite structures

Hermès Rive Gauche, Paris, France, 2010

Architecture: RDAI
Engineering: Bollinger Grohmann Ingenieure

For the biggest Hermès store that opened in Paris in 2010 the interdisciplinary team designed three nine-metre high wooden sculptures with diagonally intersecting wooden slats (Figures 14.4–14.6). The bent, glue-laminated elements are bolted together and form a diagonal grid that densifies towards the top due to the global geometry. Additional elements are introduced in the grid at different heights depending on structural and spatial requirements.

Figure 14.4–14.6

The Hermès Rive Gauche during and after construction on site.

to become an interesting alternative to solid timber construction. 'However, these require even more strictly rationalised floor plans and are mostly laid out for very regular and short spans', says Jan Knippers. Such tight constraints are not much different for solid timber plate buildings. He continues: 'Geometric diversity and complexity are topics that have not yet been adopted by timber construction for office and residential buildings'.

The situation is not much different for more familiar structural systems, even when developed with the help of computational tools. As a result of the industrialisation that drove timber construction to what it is today, truss structures are still designed in such a way that by using complex steel connectors, the geometry of timber beams is kept simple. Using the example of the Jübergturm Jan Knippers explains how the glued-laminated timber lamellas connect to the steel platforms. 'Instead of twisting the lamellas to match the connection angle, the timber beams are kept straight and the geometric complexity in the connection is shifted to custom steel details', he says. There is an evident gap between the scientific research in digital fabrication and commercial projects. Even in the case of innovative engineering companies that are continually investigating new fabrication possibilities, at the end of the day, finances make the final decision. 'Double-curved glued-laminated timber beams are currently not feasible with reasonable effort', says Jan Knippers. The Jübergturm project is still an ideal example for the collaboration between architects and engineers. The design of the thin diagonally oriented rods carrying the steel platforms are the result of an entirely digital workflow from the initial design, to structural analysis, and production. And it turns out that such a collaborative workflow is still relatively uncommon today.

Rethinking design workflows

NEW fabrication technology may not be readily available for timber construction as it is in other industrial sectors. In recent years, however, software innovation has had a more notable impact on how architects, engineers, and manufacturers collaborate during early design phases. It might turn out to be the key-stone in a profound paradigm change in the building industry. Both Grohmann and Knippers agree that computational design strategies have changed the way involved stakeholders work together in an architectural project. Compared to the traditional top-down workflow, architects and engineers can now work side by side. 'For geometrically ambitious projects, we really collaborate much more closely with architects. But our ambition is to get in contact as soon as possible even when working on more regular geometries. We understand this as a truly integrative process', says Grohmann. He sees a lot of potential in the currently emerging digital planning strategies. 'Not only BIM [building information modelling], but a coordinated 3D planning process will let architects and engineers work together from the earliest design stages. This will surely be a paradigm change', he adds.

The same principle applies for the collaboration with manufacturers. When engaging in new fabrication technologies, engineers want to integrate timber manufacturing companies in an early design stage. To elaborate on the current challenges, Jan Knippers compares the European

Jübergturm, Hemer, Germany, 2010

Architecture: Birk Heilmeyer und Frenzel
Engineering: Knippers Helbig Engineering

The 23 metre high look-out tower was designed and built for the regional horticultural festival in Hemer, Germany (Figure 14.7). The general shape is based on a hyperboloid with straight glued laminated timber members reaching from top to bottom (Figure 14.8). These timber elements carry the steel platforms inside the tower and based on necessary structural performance, they gradually densify towards the bottom. In combination with interior members oriented in the other direction, the timber members form a stable triangular structure (Figure 14.9).

Figure 14.7–14.9
The Jübergturm during and after construction.

and North American model for design processes: 'A strong hierarchical process that is common in Germany – by this we mean first the design, then the call for bids – is counterproductive for the development of strategic collaborations between architects, engineers and manufacturers. More integrated design strategies, like the design/build system wherein engineers and manufacturers collaborate closely from the start, will be necessary.' Grohmann strongly agrees on that point. The more complex a project is, the more the engineers rely on specific know-how from manufacturers and contractors, and the more they depend on their collaboration.

This is the point where architecture profoundly differs from other industries, as for example the automotive sector. An auto-manufacturer works top-down from first the concept then to the final product, combining the roles of designer, engineer, manufacturer and contractor. In comparison, an architectural project is at first designed by a multi-disciplinary team and then put out for bids. This step constitutes an important change in the project, since the responsibility gets transferred to the contracted construction company. 'That's why a seamless digital workflow will be of critical importance. It allows for construction companies to be involved as early as possible in order to influence how the project gets developed', Grohmann argues. Ultimately, integrative computational design processes will be essential in order to enable new fabrication technology to influence the design process. Without a direct digital workflow, an integration of design, structure, fabrication, and responsibilities will not be possible on a larger scale.

Rethinking material potentials

MATERIAL-ORIENTED design is the foundation of engineering, but it is especially relevant in the context of timber construction; where the material characteristics have the potential to influence the way building systems are developed. Although the discussed innovations in design and fabrication are evident, neither Grohmann nor Knippers will claim that a fundamental change in architecture has taken place in recent years. In their opinion, only a few architects are making use of the technology in a material-oriented design process, while most architectural practices still work in a traditional, form-motivated process. Grohmann however points out how the choice of material can impact the design, using the example of the Ecumenical Motorway Church Siegerland: 'At the beginning of the design process, the function and programme are discussed before the question of material comes into play. The general idea of the church and its silhouette was there from the beginning. Once a decision was made about the material, its specific characteristics and constraints play an important role for the design. The detailed geometry, such as the folded roof, as well as the spatial quality of the interior are direct implications of the decision on materials.'

Ecumenical Motorway Church, Siegerland, Germany, 2013

Architecture: schneider+schumacher
Engineering: Bollinger Grohmann Ingenieure

This church at a motorway rest stop is characterised by its abstract exterior shape and fluid interior space (Figures 14.7 and 14.8). While the silhouette was designed to resemble the church drawing on motorway signs, its construction is made of prefabricated lightweight timber frame panels. The interior is constructed from a grid made from wood panels that are cut out to describe a spherical volume. Through special shafts, daylight is guided into the church at specific angles (Figure 14.9).

Figure 14.10–14.12
The Ecumenical Motorway Church during and after construction.

The architectural quality of wood is evident for Grohmann and Knippers. Even with the available technology, however, the market share of timber construction in the building industry is not as sizeable as its potential would suggest. Grohmann explains the discrepancy with an economical perspective: 'When considering the same structural-physical requirements, timber construction is still more expensive than standard construction techniques, such as external thermal insulation composite systems for brick buildings'. More importantly, he points out that, 'Investors often say: there are timber houses, and there are normal houses'. In his opinion, a lack of confidence, experience, and an outdated understanding of the material are prevalent reasons why wood architecture has not been able to develop its full potential in central Europe.

When facing future environmental challenges, however, timber construction promises to be the only truly sustainable building material and therefore holds a special incentive for decision makers during the design process. By binding carbon dioxide during its growth, trees are responsible for an important long-term CO_2 storage. Thus, using as much wood as possible would be the natural consequence as long as sufficient supplies are available. At first glance this argument seems to contradict the ambitions of engineers to design lightweight structures with a minimum of material. Nevertheless, this question can be resolved when viewed from another angle: 'For engineers, "efficiency" is the key word', says Knippers, with Grohmann adding: 'There is no real contradiction between these two points of view. When building with slender timber frame constructions, all other constructional layers (such as the insulation) have to fill the remaining voids between the beams, and therefore get divided into multiple smaller pieces. Effectively, many more vapour barriers, plastic films, and sealants are needed. This complexity stands in contrast to cross laminated timber panels, where a clear division between construction layers simplifies the overall production and assembly process.' Evidently, intricate and complex details in timber construction transcend the fabrication constraints of wood processing alone and influence other trades involved in building construction, making it an interdisciplinary problem.

Ultimately, the contradictory relationship between lightweight and solid timber construction represents the challenge that wood architecture is currently facing. Developments in computational design and digital fabrication techniques bring architects, engineers, and manufacturers closer together, and enable them to break free from both standardised production processes and conventional construction techniques. However, each individual development necessitates a certain technological standard for all involved actors and is therefore in close reciprocal relation with other sectors of the building industry. As Grohmann and Knippers point out, economic requirements will stand in the way of a true paradigm change as long as not all industrial sectors have adopted a digitalised design and fabrication process. Complex yet efficient construction systems will not be feasible if the necessary fabrication technology is not available, but even if it is, they will need to be made an integrative part of the design process.

After having worked with wood for several decades, Manfred Grohmann and Jan Knippers clearly see its potential for the future. Based on a sustainable, efficient and locally available building material, advanced wood architecture has already adopted the image of an innovation leader within the building industry. However, it will take more time and effort to truly reveal the potentials of timber construction.

Acknowledgements

Tʜɪs article is based on two interviews with Manfred Grohmann and Jan Knippers. The names of the speakers are mentioned in connection with their excerpts. Passages may have been slightly edited for clarity and to represent the interviewees' position.

– 15 –

Architectural perspectives

Axel Kilian

School of Architecture, Princeton University, USA

T͟H͟E potential for material- and technology-driven changes in timber architecture is large and is being explored in academic research, including projects presented at the *Advancing Wood Architecture* Symposium at the German Architecture Museum in Frankfurt (27 March 2015). However, how exactly fundamental research ties back into building practice and whether results can be implemented in the field of architecture before they are adopted by other industries and potentially exploited in trivial ways appears less clear. Matthias Kohler, Achim Menges, Yves Weinand, Jeremy Ralph, and guest-critic Johan Bettum of Staedelschule, Frankfurt, shared their views on the future of timber architecture in a roundtable discussion that concluded the symposium. In his contribution, Axel Kilian (who led the discussion) aggregates the different views into an architectural perspective on the relation between technology and architecture, including such diverse topics as complexity (of design, natural process and technology), interdisciplinarity, resource systems, research processes, theoretical discourse, aesthetics, and design thinking. The different positions in the discussion reflect the title of the symposium as not only a call to push the field forward, but also as a reminder to critically reflect on the research trajectories and the relation between technology and architecture.

The complexity of natural processes versus the technology complex

T͟H͟E role of research and experimentation in developing novel approaches in architectural design plays a central role in the work of the research institutes and the individual contributors of the symposium. Within the discourse, wood took on the role of a catalyst for bringing out new exemplary approaches to material use and fabrication processes. Most of the institutes engage in other material research and processes besides wood, but as one of the oldest materials in architecture, revisiting its use from a computational perspective seems particularly promising. Applying new technology to established processes offers a rich experimentation field and productive tensions between traditional craft-based knowledge and the need to externalize and re-implement

Figure 15.1

Discussion panel at the *Advancing Wood Architecture* Symposium in March 2015.

tacit material knowledge, a complex, which Achim Menges referred to as 'material culture'. Johan Bettum, in turn, believes that in the future, material culture will not be anything like material culture today, but that it is difficult to unseat the established ways of thinking.

In Yves Weinand's words, the challenge is to learn from traditional material use precedents and translate them into today's technology context, as presented in his work. This will entail a critical re-evaluation of the resource streams around wood use in construction and can even be used generatively, as shown by Jeremy Ralph and the Design & Make group in their presentation on Hooke Park. According to Matthias Kohler, another challenge is the danger of getting stuck in a potentially naïve back-to-nature approach that ignores the global resource realities. From an architectural perspective, he finds it problematic to return to a purely romantic view of nature and thus miss out on the benefits of new technologies for architecture today. He believes in the potential of new technologies to empower local players in an economical and industrial sense. Achim Menges points out that the materials and resources necessary to realize projects such as the Institute for Computational Design at the University of Stuttgart's HygroScope project have been available for years, which in turn made Matthias Kohler pose the question, 'What is it that is limiting us today in our technological performance- and optimization-driven world?'

In response, Johan Bettum posited that it may be optimization itself that holds us back. Beyond technical and economic implications, Achim Menges emphasized that technological advances not only expand the possibilities of material use, but also shift our design thinking. The increasing interest and understanding of the complexity of natural systems goes hand in hand with a push to evolve increasingly complex artificial systems of technology that are driven by incorporating the physical world through sensing and actuation and interface with the realm of computational models.

Evolving interdisciplinary models

THERE are increasing overlaps between disciplines in the use of technology and their under-lying models of abstraction in the form of code and computational infrastructure. Industrial robotic arms are an example of technology first being adopted by one sector (the manufacturing industry) but now being used by another sector (architectural research) in a way that is pushing forward new experimental usage scenarios that are of interest to the robotics industry. Overlaps in the use of robotic hardware and finding common modes of operating between engineering and architecture have created new links to industry. No discipline operates in isolation and the cycle of adaptation and absorption of knowledge is speeding up.

Architectural and engineering creativity in exploring these techniques has created a unique opportunity of being at the forefront of the development of material computational systems. Achim Menges referred to this as a type of cyber-physical production system, which is a term used in manufacturing industries to denote a system where the computational, material and physical domains merge. This is a research characteristic that connects all the participants in the symposium. Johan Bettum emphasized in his response that most of the work is still in the realm of fundamental research, but that research has come so far already that industry collaborations begin to develop. While stating that technology is here to stay, he also pointed out that simply making use of technology does not warrant any attention by itself.

Compared to the complexity of the physical world, the number of robustly implemented computational models remains relatively small. So there is necessarily an hour glass effect, where the physical world is abstracted and reduced through sensing and encoding in data and then for reasoning and designing expanded back out on the computational side. The narrow available technology tunnel is in many ways constrained by industry standards and the invention of new processes. If architectural research does not take an active role in developing computational processes for its own needs, it will always be dependent on the existing interdisciplinary models. A strong research culture allows for stronger industry relations, potentially influencing developments that exceed the possibilities of the current context of architecture in academia and practice. But while such interdisciplinary approaches are crucial, they can also lead to a loss of critical distance that is crucial in guiding research work.

Hi-technology versus low technology

WHAT then guides and motivates the use of the technology and how does one ensure a critical approach while making a meaningful impact on architecture? Matthias Kohler stresses the importance of the attitude towards these processes and resources as a key topic in today's society, while not neglecting how our world is actually working globally today. Yves Weinand points out that wood use in architecture is evolving thanks to engineered wood products that are occasionally already competitive with established construction materials such as concrete, even in contemporary five storey administrative buildings. While it is important not to forget that five story wood buildings were already accomplished in the seventeenth century, they were produced under different standards of regulations and comfort.

Architecture is changing with the advances in research-driven processes of design and material-specific design and fabrication. The changes occur both in high tech and low tech solutions, but also hybrid ones where technology helps to apply low tech solutions in a new architectural context or scale. Examples are the traditional Japanese wood joining techniques being applied at an architectural scale in Yves Weinand's group or the stacking of three dimensionally scanned non-straight tree trunks into the curved wall of the biomass house at Hooke Park. Yet surprisingly many of the historic wood construction examples shown by Yves Weinand share similarities to today's robotic experimentations despite being developed under very different resource constraints. It may be the case that the very limited possibilities of the time required a more integrated material approach. Today's technological development is in many ways similar in its limitation based on the still simplistic integration of sensing and knowledge of the world. Compared to a crafts person's knowledge and awareness of the physical world he or she works in, the perspective through the technological lens is still very limited and this limitation may produce similar constraints in the technological experiments of today compared to the resource constraints of traditional examples. One can view the entire resource cycle as an integrated system, where through sensing and technology, we slowly learn to regain some of the sensibilities of material use and balancing of resources that were lost with the advances in mechanization. But it cannot be simply a return to the historic crafts, as the challenges we are facing have also evolved with population growth and a global economy and higher standards of living and comfort. As Achim Menges states, the design systems that are being developed now where computers connect to the physical world open up different approaches to design thinking.

Theoretical discourse versus architectural relevance

So how can research be directed to stay relevant and remain within the architectural discourse and design culture? The theoretical discourse is an important part of history and theory in architecture, but at times there is a disparity between the technological depth necessary to progress technology-driven research and the contextualization necessary for theoretical reflection.

Architectural practice rarely offers enough time and resources to engage in fundamental research and the theoretical discourse often develops in parallel or after the work has been created. This potential divide between theoretical discourse and its architectural relevance was a further point of debate in the discussion. Matthias Kohler commented that there is a need to develop a deep understanding and consistency in the way these new technologies are used. Additionally, he observes a shift in sensibilities in the design culture of a young generation of architects that goes beyond the use of technology in a purely functionalist manner. Instead it focuses on creativity, limiting the risk that other industries that focus on technological aspects will move in and take over. Achim Menges concurs, stressing that this is one of the few situations where designers and architects are at the forefront of thinking about technological possibilities and their impact, and therefore can shape the discourse, which includes events like the *Advancing Wood Architecture* Symposium. He argues that the detailed technological discourse is necessary because it is often disregarded in other venues and the main focus is on the outcomes or the effects that are achieved. He thinks it is essential to understand the depth of the processes and the little steps that are necessary to actually get to a point where one can discuss the research at an architectural level. Jeremy Ralph raised the point whether the focus on the theoretical discourse may contribute to architecture being left behind while the construction industry is increasingly engaging wood based technologies in architectural production. In his opinion, what should be the focus is how to get the research findings to be used in real architecture. Johan Bettum vehemently defended the essential need for discussion and talk about architectural design as the very core that sets up the discipline of architecture. It is apparent that a technology-aware theoretical discourse is developing that is pushing for architectural relevance of the experimental projects currently developing at many architecture schools. It is crucial to develop a criticality that can reflect the nuances of long term technological development and guide its development while avoiding the -ism trap, as the challenges are too large and the potential too big to dismiss the development as simply a style driven debate. The discourse touches on the very core of the relationship of architecture to its material realm and the design processes that govern its existence. But the research processes and research interests continue to evolve and what was presented at the symposium is unlikely to be representative of the domain in only a few years' time.

Changes in the research processes

WHAT do the research processes look like in more detail and how do they evolve? One difference mentioned by Achim Menges is the shift from knowledge based systems to behaviour based systems, such as in the example of the HygroScope wood louvers. Rather than incorporating more and more material knowledge in computational models, the proposal is to base the work less on assumptions of how things are but rather on observations of the actual material behaviour. He argues that morphological models and principles developed at the ICD have a lot of intricacy, which is very appropriate for wood, as we have lost more than we can comprehend when dealing with purely geometric design processes. He says that digital technologies offer the great opportunity to access parts of the design space previously not accessible and to work with the complex behaviour of wood, no longer being bound by the standards of fabrication processes but designing the fabrication process itself. For Achim Menges computation opens up the design perspective: we need to understand the enabling technologies on a profound level and may have to re-teach our aesthetic sensibilities and value systems. For Matthias Kohler, the development goes in the direction where you have clearly adaptive fabrication technology that enables one to adapt to different systems and materials for assembly and on the fly production. He sees a great potential to improve on the materialization of architecture and to add to the quality of our built environment. He hopes that these qualities can be unlocked through the diversity of research conducted by the Gramazio Kohler research group. Matthias Kohler sees the timber industry as an early adopter of digital technologies that could act as a role model for other construction industry sectors, such as the concrete or the steel industry. He is optimistic that a contemporary building culture is emerging that goes beyond the current status quo in building logistics and optimization and, further, that the integration of robotic technologies offers the possibility to empower local industries.

Design thinking and architectural aesthetics

D ESIGN thinking is changing and the effects on the architectural results also bring up the question of the aesthetic dimension of the work. Johan Bettum raised the point that across the work of the different presenters of the symposium, the results look like they are guided by an aesthetic that is representative and specific to the group of presenters and might not be directly guided by material-specific morphological criteria but may rather stem from design decisions and parameters set up beforehand. These a priori decisions that go into the setup of the experiments influence the architectural outcomes. Also Johan Bettum doubts that embedding ourselves in every material flow can or ever will dictate the entire outcome and that this is where he struggles to understand the relation of the presented research to architecture and design. Yves Weinand sees open research fields in architecture even in the low tech possibilities of massive timber or in the renewed interest in beech wood, which has traditionally not been used as a building material due to its tendency to warp. With today's beech based panels and applications with layer thicknesses of 3mm, he sees new possibilities of wood use in the architectural context. But as technology opens up new possibilities in using wood, the danger is also to reduce these changes simply to technology making processes more efficient. Achim Menges views the efficiency dialogue as fundamentally problematic and avoids the term explicitly and instead prefers to speak of effectiveness. It is very easy to be caught up in making things more efficient in the context of technology but he refers to the following definition to distinguish the two terms – 'efficiency is doing things right and effectiveness is doing the right thing'. This is a reminder to remain critical in the development of technological approaches and not lose what distinguishes the profession from other disciplines and industries that are much more adept at absorbing technological progress, but may do so in the most trivial manner. Johan Bettum also cautioned against viewing technological progress through the lens of optimization as the optimization itself may turn out to be the limiting factor in going forward.

Looking at the architectural projects in the research presentations, one can sense the fine balance between the frugal excess of the robotically assembled wooden truss roof of the Institute for Technology in Architecture by Gramazio Kohler research; the critical response to globally shipped wood products in the form of the renewed interest of Hooke Park in its local forest as wood supply and the interest to let the architectural form be informed by what is found on site; the material and biomimetic driven design developments of ICD, which convince in their conceptual and implementation precision and their interdisciplinary approach; and Yves Weinand's group whose work gives hope for a strong resurgence of computationally and technologically empowered craft at an architectural scale.

Computational processes function as an enabling technology, but they are clearly driven by a research passion to prove that change can be brought about and novel industrial processes and architectural aesthetics are within reach. At best, we only saw a glimpse of what is possible in the near future. At its worst, the technology development may become a form of access control to architectural implementation, similar to other industries that have gone through excessive consolidation and streamlined production processes. But the most powerful argument against this scenario is the strong bottom-up individual research culture that exists within and in parallel to the represented research institutes that in many cases are crucial enablers through their open source contributions and ground breaking research.

Acknowledgments

Tʜɪs text was developed around excerpts from the audio transcript of the closing roundtable discussion of the *Advancing Wood Architecture* Symposium at the German Architecture Museum, Frankfurt (27 March 2015). The names of the speakers are mentioned in connection with their excerpts and passages may have been slightly altered for clarity and to represent the panellists' different positions within the overall text by the author.

ADVANCING WOOD ARCHITECTURE
new computational perspectives

Roundtable Discussion

with Johan Bettum, Matthias Kohler, Achim Menges,
Jeremy Ralph, and Yves Weinand. Moderated by Axel Kilian.

Aleksandra Anna Apolinarska is a researcher at Gramazio Kohler Research at the ETH Zürich. After graduating in Architecture from Poznan University of Technology and University of Stuttgart, she worked for various architectural offices across Europe, including Foster+Partners, designtoproduction, LAVA and UNStudio, specialising in computational design of complex geometries. Since 2013 Aleksandra Anna Apolinarska is responsible for the development of the 'Sequential Roof' project.

Olivier Baverel is Professor at the National School of Architecture in Grenoble (France), Professor adj. at the Ecole des Ponts ParisTech, and a research fellow of the Laboratoire Navier (UMR ENPC/IFSTTAR/CNRS, France). His research activities cover aspects of behaviour, analysis and design of lightweight structures, with emphasis on problems of geometrically nonlinear behaviour, form-finding and structural optimisation for elastic gridshells and reciprocal systems or nexorades. He is also, since 2012, editor of the *International Journal of Space Structures*.

Fabio Gramazio is an architect with multi-disciplinary interests ranging from computational design and robotic fabrication to material innovation. In 2000, he founded the architecture practice Gramazio Kohler Architects in conjunction with his partner Matthias Kohler, where numerous award-wining designs have been realised. Opening also the world's first architectural robotic laboratory at ETH Zürich, Fabio Gramazio's and Matthias Kohler's research has been formative in the field of digital architecture, setting precedence and de facto creating a new research field, merging advanced architectural design and additive fabrication processes through the customised use of industrial robots. This ranges from 1:1 prototype installations to the design of robotically fabricated high-rises. His work has been published in many journals, books and media, and was first documented in the book *Digital Materiality in Architecture* (2008).

Volker Helm specialised in computer aided architectural design at ETH Zürich after successfully completing his studies in architecture at the University of Siegen (Germany). He subsequently worked for six years at the Herzog & de Meuron architectural office in Basel, specialising in the development, programming and realisation of complex geometries. Since 2010, Volker Helm has been working with Professor Fabio Gramazio and Professor Matthias Kohler as a research associate at ETH Zürich. Since 2013 he has been responsible for coordinating the research of the group. In 2015, he completed his doctoral degree which focuses on potentials of on-site robotic construction, under the supervision of Prof. Dr. Georg Trogemann (Academy of Media Arts in Cologne) and Prof. Matthias Kohler (Chair of Architecture and Digital Fabrication at ETH Zürich).

Axel Kilian is an Assistant Professor at the Princeton University School of Architecture. He previously taught Computational Design at the Department of Architecture at MIT and at TU Delft. In 2006 he completed a PhD in Design and Computation at MIT on design exploration. In addition he holds a Master of Science from MIT and a professional degree in architecture from the University of the Arts Berlin. Axel Kilian has lectured widely and published extensively. His publications include *Architectural Geometry* (2007) and he has been involved in many conference series such as SmartGeometry, Design Modelling Symposium, and Advances in Architectural Geometry. His latest research focus is on embodied computation, the continuation of computation in the physical realm.

Michael Knauss is an architect and researcher based in Zurich, Switzerland. He studied architecture at the ETH Zürich and the University of Stuttgart where he graduated in 2007. Michael gained professional experience in the offices of UNStudio (Amsterdam) and LAVA (Stuttgart). He is a founding partner of the architectural practice ROK – Rippmann Oesterle Knauss GmbH. As researcher and project leader at Gramazio & Kohler Research, ETH Zürich, he focused on additive robotic timber construction. He was responsible for the development of the 'Sequential Roof' and the NRP66 research project 'Additive Robotic Fabrication of Complex Timber Structures'.

Matthias Kohler is an architect with multi-disciplinary interests ranging from computational design and robotic fabrication to material innovation. In 2000, he founded the architecture practice Gramazio Kohler Architects in conjunction with his partner Fabio Gramazio, where numerous award-wining designs have been realised. Opening also the world's first architectural robotic laboratory at ETH Zürich, Matthias Kohler's research has been formative in the field of digital architecture, setting precedence and de facto creating a new research field merging advanced architectural design and additive fabrication processes through the customised use of industrial robots. Since 2014, Matthias Kohler is also director of the new National Centre of Competence in Research (NCCR) Digital Fabrication.

Thomas Kohlhammer graduated first in civil engineering (2000) and afterwards in architecture (2004), both at the University of Stuttgart. Simultaneously he collaborates in several research projects at the University of Stuttgart. As of 2000 he gained practical experience in architecture and civil engineering offices in Stuttgart and Zurich. From 2005 to 2009 he worked as research and teaching assistant at the Chair of Structural Design, ETH Zürich. From 2009 to 2013 he did a PHD at the ETH Zürich (Prof. Dr. Joseph Schwartz). Since 2009 he has a lectureship in Structural Design at the Department of Architecture at the Lucerne University of Applied Sciences and Arts. Since 2013 he has his own architecture office and works additionally as research fellow at the Chair of Architecture and Digital Fabrication (Prof. Fabio Gramazio, Prof. Matthias Kohler), ETH Zürich.

Oliver David Krieg is a research associate and doctoral candidate at the Institute for Computational Design at the University of Stuttgart. With the completion of his Diploma degree in 2012 he also received the faculty's Diploma Price. Prior to that, he was working as a Graduate Assistant at the institute's robotic prototype laboratory since the beginning of 2010. With a profound interest in computational design processes and digital fabrication in architecture, he participated in several award winning and internationally published research projects. In the context of computational design his research aims to investigate the architectural potentials of robotic fabrication in wood construction.

Achim Menges is a registered architect and professor at the University of Stuttgart where he is the founding director of the Institute for Computational Design. Currently he is also Visiting Professor in Architecture at Harvard University's Graduate School of Design and Visiting Professor of the Emergent Technologies and Design Graduate Programme at the Architectural Association, London. Achim Menges' research and practice focuses on the development of integrative design processes at the intersection of morphogenetic design computation, biomimetic engineering and digital fabrication. His projects and design research has received numerous international awards, and has been published and exhibited worldwide.

Sina Nabaei is a structural engineer and graduated from the École Nationale des Ponts et Chaussées Paris. From 2007–2009, he contributed to the structural design of glass canopies of the Fondation Louis Vuitton in Paris. In 2014, he completed his PhD on form-finding of timber fabric structures at the École polytechnique Fédérale de Lausanne, where he explored computational approaches to deal with the nonlinear equilibrium of elastic interlaced panels. His field of expertise is on complex geometry, form-active structures and Bridge/Infrastructure engineering. He is currently working at BG Consulting Engineers Lausanne.

Christopher Robeller is an architect and postdoctoral researcher at the Timber Construction Laboratory IBOIS at EPFL Lausanne. Christopher received his architecture diploma with distinction from London Metropolitan University in 2008 and worked at the Institute for Computational Design, Stuttgart from 2008–2010, where he developed integral timber plate joints for the award-winning ICD/ITKE Research Pavilion 2010. Since 2011 he has been working at IBOIS and received a doctoral degree from EPFL in 2015 for his thesis entitled 'Integral Mechanical Attachment for Timber Folded Plate Structures'. His research was published in journals and conferences such as *Bauingenieur*, ACADIA, RobArch and AAG, where he received the Best Paper Award 2014.

Martin Self is Director of Hooke Park, the Architectural Association's woodland campus for research in timber architecture, and Director of the MArch Design & Make programme. He holds degrees in aerospace engineering and architecture theory, and worked as a consultant engineer at Ove Arup & Partners between 1996 and 2007 where he was a founding member of its Advanced Geometry Group. He has also consulted within practices including Zaha Hadid Architects and Antony Gormley Studio. He has taught at the Architectural Association since 2005 and directed Hooke Park since 2010 where he is overseeing the production of a series of student-designed experimental buildings.

Tobias Schwinn is research associate and doctoral candidate at the Institute for Computational Design (ICD) at the University of Stuttgart, Germany. In his research he focuses on the integration of robotic fabrication and computational design processes. Prior to joining the ICD in January 2011, he worked as a Senior Designer for Skidmore, Owings and Merrill in New York and London applying computational design techniques to parametric form-finding, rationalisation, complex geometry, automation and environmental design. Tobias studied architecture at the Bauhaus-University in Weimar, Germany and at the University of Pennsylvania in Philadelphia as part of the US–EU Joint Consortium for Higher Education. He received his diploma-engineering degree in architecture in 2005.

Glen Stellmacher is a designer from Seattle, USA. He is a graduate of the University of Washington, and the Architectural Association School of Architecture's MArch Design & Make Programme. Here, he was responsible, along with three others, for the design and delivery of the Timber Seasoning Shelter, was a finalist for the 2014 UK Wood Awards, and has published widely internationally. Glen has lectured at the Welsh School of Architecture, and helped teach workshops in digital design and fabrication at Hooke Park. He has worked with Kengo Kuma Architects in Tokyo, and is currently forming his own studio based in Seattle.

Yingzi Wang is a current MArch Design & Make student at Hooke Park, the Architectural Association's woodland campus. Yingzi has also studied architecture in China and Taiwan, and was a key member of D[a]L (Digital Architecture Lab) at Hunan University. She was involved in the Komorebi Workshop by ZHA code, 'Mechanic Materiality' international conference and workshop, and an academic exchange with Taiwan Tunghai University. She has practiced in URBANUS; Shenzhen office. Currently, along with her partner, she is exploring the architectural possibilities between 3D scanning technologies and naturally crooked timber, through designing and building the Biomass Boiler House at Hooke Park.

Yves Weinand is an architect and structural engineer and founder of the Bureau d'Études Weinand in Liège/Belgium. He is currently working on the ice rink in Liège and the parliament building in Lausanne, where timber is used as the structural component. Since 2004 he has been Professor and Head of IBOIS Laboratory for timber constructions at the EPFL. Here he directs an interdisciplinary group of architects, engineers, mathematicians and computer scientists who perform research work in the fields of timber rib shells, folded timber plate structures and woven timber structures.

Jan Willmann is Senior Research Assistant at the Chair of Architecture and Digital Fabrication at ETH Zürich. He studied architecture in Liechtenstein, Oxford and Innsbruck where he received his PhD degree in 2010. Previously, from 2007 to 2010, he was a research assistant and lecturer at the Chair of Architectural Theory of Professor Ir. Bart Lootsma and gained professional experience in numerous architectural offices as an architect and consultant. He co-founded the platform Architekturtheorie.eu and participated in a number of international research and exhibition projects His research focuses on digital architecture and its theoretical implications as a composed computational and material score. As such, he has lectured internationally at various universities and published extensively, including *The Robotic Touch – How Robots Change Architecture* (2014), the first anthology of robots in architecture.